PLAYWRIGHTS—LIKE PLAYS—
AREN'T BORN BUT MADE

"Paradoxically, though a person probably can't be taught to be a writer, a writer can learn to become a playwright. This book is filled with a great deal of wisdom about the craft of writing a play, and, equally important, a great deal of information on what to do with it once it is written." —Robert Anderson, author of *I Never Sang for My Father* and *Tea and Sympathy*

"Concise and well presented . . . I highly recommend it."
—Elizabeth McCann, Broadway producer

"The authors cover everything from finding the right workshop to join to the complex mechanics of playwrighting."
—*Los Angeles Times Book Review*

Now you can find out how a play and a playwright are made—with this definitive guide that offers instruction, information, and inspiration to both beginning and professional playwrights.

THE PLAYWRIGHT'S HANDBOOK

FRANK PIKE is an award-winning playwright who had been a faculty member at the University of Minnesota and Middlebury College. He has received grants from the Mellon Foundation, the Bush Foundation, and the Jerome Foundation. He is co-author (with Thomas G. Dunn) of *Scenes and Monologues From the New American Theater*, available in a Mentor edition.

THOMAS G. DUNN, in addition to being a noted director and playwright, is Artistic Director of the New Tradition and of Heartland Plays, and founder of the prestigious Minnesota Playwrights Center.

THE PLAYWRIGHT'S HANDBOOK

REVISED AND UPDATED EDITION

FRANK PIKE & THOMAS G. DUNN

PLUME
Published by the Penguin Group
Penguin Books USA Inc., 375 Hudson Street,
New York, New York 10014, U.S.A.
Penguin Books Ltd, 27 Wrights Lane,
London W8 5TZ, England
Penguin Books Australia Ltd, Ringwood,
Victoria, Australia
Penguin Books Canada Ltd, 10 Alcorn Avenue,
Toronto, Ontario, Canada M4V 3B2
Penguin Books (N.Z.) Ltd, 182–190 Wairau Road,
Auckland 10, New Zealand

Penguin Books Ltd, Registered Offices:
Harmondsworth, Middlesex, England

First published by Plume, an imprint of Dutton Signet,
a division of Penguin Books USA Inc.

First Printing, July, 1985
First Printing (Revised and Updated Edition), April, 1996
10 9 8 7 6 5 4 3

LIBRARY OF CONGRESS CATALOGING-IN-PUBLICATION DATA
Pike, Frank.
The playwright's handbook.
1. Playwriting. I. Dunn, Thomas G. II. Title.
PN1661.P54 1985 808'.02 85-318
ISBN 0-452-27588-1

Printed in the United States of America

ACKNOWLEDGMENTS

The authors would like to thank the following:

The Andrew Mellon Foundation, Spencer Beckwith, The Bush Foundation, Aija Brigance, The Children's Theatre (Minnesota), Jeanne Cowan, Ted Crawford, Nancy Erickson, Eileen Fallon, Barbara Field (and some eighty playwrights who have been in residence at the Playwrights' Center or members of New Dramatists over the last ten years), Louise Gittelson, Amy Hinds, The Jerome Foundation, Jean Kram, Lea Ann Le Tourneau, David LeVine, Mary Lucas, Jennifer Mohr, Dr. Charles Nolte, Claudia Reilly, Lloyd Richards, Kirk Ristau, Susan Schulman, Dr. Douglas Sprigg, Dr. Thomas F. Van Laan, and Heidi Jo Edwards. Finally, Tom Dunn would like to dedicate this book to Louise Williams—a playwright, a teacher, a scholar, and a person who lived and breathed playwriting during her too short life.

CONTENTS

INTRODUCTION

The Playwright's Handbook is a complete training manual and survival guide for anyone who is interested in writing for the theater. The book helps you take full advantage of a recent revolution in playwriting: *the workshop approach*. The workshop approach is a method of developing both new plays and new playwrights in an efficient, *step-by-step* process—systematic, simple, and sane.

Before the advent of the workshop approach in the late 1960s, the development of new plays and new playwrights was, for the most part, haphazard, a matter of trial and error and luck, usually under the worst possible circumstances. Budding playwrights often took classes where the emphasis was on the play as literature, not theater. The method of teaching was little more than telling the aspiring playwright: "Go home and write a play, bring it in, and the class will talk about it as a group." With little or no idea what playwriting was about, the would-be playwright went home, floundered around, and came back with several dozen pages of a "play" —a huge, ungainly, overwhelming, dull thing. Confronted with a play riddled with problems, the class discussion frequently ended up general, aimless, usually more harmful than helpful for the aspiring playwright, who needed detailed, *specific* criticism of *specific* problem areas.

For those who survived trying to learn the fundamentals of playwriting and eventually did write a play worthy of production, an even worse fate awaited.

The play went into rehearsal, usually with an opening slated four to eight weeks later—sometimes less. Then chaos ensured. On the second day of rehearsal, the playwright realized that the great moment between Lenny and Bruce at the end of Act One, which he or she had imagined as fantastic onstage, was all wrong; that the character of Aunt Ophelia should be trimmed, perhaps even cut altogether; that maybe the setting for the last scene should be a nightclub, not a Dairy Queen after all, and so on.

A hundred little things invariably needed fixing. Fix one thing, and two other things needed fixing—a virtual Gorgon's head of rewriting. Panicked, the playwright began rewriting. By the second week, the play had been slashed and hacked and turned upside down and inside out so much that the playwright could hardly remember the name of the play, much less what it was about. But the play opened in less than two weeks. To delay the opening, even a week, would kill the theater; the production was already over budget. Besides, the posters had been up since Wednesday. So, another cup of coffee, and it was back to writing against the clock, cutting and pasting, taking shortcuts, pulling old tricks out of the theatrical trunk . . .

Read the biographies, memoirs, and notebooks of master American playwrights such as Tennessee Williams and Eugene O'Neill, whose heydays were before the advent of the workshop approach, and you'll see the playwright's enormous frustration with a system that hindered rather than enhanced the initial production of their new plays. Little wonder playwriting in America began to flounder in the late 1950s and early 1960s.

Small, experimental theater groups in New York and elsewhere across the country, seeking to remedy what was beginning to look like a hopeless situation, developed the workshop approach, both to develop new plays and train new playwrights. The workshop approach treats playwriting as a *craft*, to be learned and developed slowly and methodically.

For the new playwright, for instance, instead of being told to "go out and write a play," *systematic* exercises allow you to learn the tools and techniques of putting a play together, piece by piece, starting from the absolute basics—learning to look at familiar places for material, developing character, using setting to your best advantage, handling conflict, and so on—and working your way *step-by-step* to the creation of a complete full-length play.

For the playwright with a new play, the workshop approach does away with the concept of the playwright laboring alone for months on end, only to notice all the problems in the play on the second day of rehearsal, then frantically rewriting in some Boston hotel room under the overwhelming pressures of an impending opening night. Instead, *systematic* steps—cold readings, nonperformance workshops, and staged readings—encourage you to work through your play, draft after draft, in collaboration with directors, actors, and designers, all in a relaxed laboratory situation, with ample time between each step for rewriting. And, with each step, your play becomes much richer, much more performance ready, each "mini-collaboration" with actors, directors, and designers providing you with invaluable feedback.

Although popular only for little more than a decade, the workshop approach, both as a means of training playwrights and developing new plays, now dominates the American theater scene, from community theaters, to college and university theaters, to regional theaters, to Off-Broadway, even the Broadway musical—*A Chorus Line*, *Nine*, *Sunday in the Park with George*, and *Passion* are recent examples of Broadway musicals developed by the workshop approach. Just when everyone was saying there were no more good American playwrights, out of the American workshop system have come Christopher Durang, Beth Henley, David Mamet, Terrence McNally, Marsha Norman, Sam Shepard, Wendy Wasserstein, August Wilson, Lanford Wilson, and many other exciting new writers, whose plays have won critical acclaim and audience support all across the country. And the American theater is clamoring for more new talent. You maybe? Why not?

The Playwright's Handbook will prove an invaluable resource and reference through your entire career as an amateur or professional playwright—from your first work with observing and recording your observations to having your play "go up" in a mainstage production.

The authors have been intimately involved with the workshop approach since the early 1970s: Frank, with training new playwrights in universities and colleges, theaters, and writers' groups across the United States; Tom, with working with "journeyman" playwrights and developing new plays in professional and semi-professional playwriting organizations, both in New York and regionally. Like most people involved with the workshop approach, both of us turned to the workshop approach out of frustration with old methods of training new playwrights and developing new plays. As participants in and observers of the workshop approach, we've been stunned by its success. We've watched people whose only experience with theater was running lights for *Oklahoma!* their senior year of high school go through the workshop system and emerge talents to be reckoned with. We've watched early drafts of plays that were considered naive, even hopeless, bloom in a workshop environment, becoming well-crafted, exciting theater pieces.

We wrote *The Playwright's Handbook* to share our collective experience and enthusiasm with as wide an audience as possible. Frank developed the first half of the book, "Building a Play," which focuses on developing the new playwright and learning how to write a play. Tom put together the second half of the book, "Being a Playwright," which focuses on workshopping and producing new plays, surviving financially, entering contests, and other concerns of the playwright in the 1990s.

Part One, "Building a Play," uses a step-by-step workshop approach to remove the mystery and confusion from learning how to write a play. Three workshops—Beginning, Intermediate, and Advanced—allow you to gradually (and, for the most part, painlessly) immerse yourself in the nuts and bolts of the craft. Starting with short, simple exercises, you learn to "build" a complete full-length play, gaining a solid grasp of the tools and techniques common to good playwriting.

The exercises in the Beginning Workshop develop basic skills, including work in observation and memory, exploring settings, creating characters, evolving relationships, and shaping conflict—all in preparation for the dramatization of an emotionally charged "moment" from your life. Building on what you learn in the Beginning Workshop, the Intermediate Workshop provides scene-length exercises, each of which focuses on a specific problem or situation often encountered in playwriting, which requires craft and ingenuity to solve. Everything comes together in the third and final workshop, the creation of a full-length play. The three workshops encourage a lot of "on your feet" work, such as observing people, exploring environments, listening to conversations, digging into your past, and so on. All "on your feet" work is linked with complementary written exercises. The three workshops emphasize, above all, *theater,* writing for the stage—for actors, directors, designers, a theater audience—learning to create exciting, vital plays.

Part Two, "Being a Playwright," is a guide for those who have written a play and want to get it workshopped and/or produced. You learn how to take advantage of the extensive professional and semiprofessional workshop system presently available in the United States. You also learn the fine art of staying alive as a playwright, making contacts, making the right moves, and making ends meet.

The first part of "Being a Playwright" illustrates the various steps of the workshop approach to new play development—the cold reading, the staged reading, the nonperformance workshop—showing you how to get the most out of each step. The emphasis is on collaboration, working closely with other theater artists to make your work the best it could possibly be. Included also is a description of the major workshop-oriented theaters, retreats, and conferences throughout the country, and what they can offer a writer with a new play.

"Being a Playwright" also shows writers living in a part of the country without a workshop-oriented theater how to set up a playwrights' workshop, either independently or in affiliation with an arts-related group.

Of special interest is a financial survival guide for the struggling playwright of the 1990s, describing monies available and how to get them, contests to enter, what kinds of supplemental jobs are best for a playwright, and so on. Other important business concerns such as finding an agent, figuring out your taxes as a writer, and handling such legal matters as contracts, options, and royalties are included in the section.

The success of the workshop approach has opened up all sorts of opportunities for training new playwrights and producing their work, in theaters at all levels, all across America. New playwrights are hot. New plays are hot. Large theaters, small theaters, professional theaters, community theaters, college theaters, conferences, contests, even film producers, are looking for good new plays to develop. A huge corps of talented actors, directors, and designers have a virtually insatiable appetite for new material they can help mold and shape. If you have never written a play, but you want to learn how, *The Playwright's Handbook* is the perfect training manual, allowing you to learn and develop *step by step,* at your own pace, all the tools, techniques, and tricks of the trade used by experienced playwrights. If you are a playwright—whether you have written one play or so many you lost count long ago, whether you're a professional or an amateur—*The Playwright's Handbook* is the perfect resouce for getting your play workshopped and/or produced.

The 1980s and 1990s have seen a renaissance for American playwriting; interest in new plays in the United States has never been keener. Opportunities for you as a playwright, both in terms of learning the craft and seeing your play performed, have never been greater. Whether you're just starting out or you have been writing for years, *The Playwright's Handbook* will help you take full advantage of the many resources available to today's playwrights.

PART ONE

BUILDING A PLAY

CHAPTER ONE
THE BEGINNING WORKSHOP

Let's start at point zero and assume you know little or nothing about the mechanics of playwriting—or even creative writing as a whole. Even if you have had some writing experience, the Beginning Workshop works best if you begin with the first step and do *every* step *in order*. Each step in the Beginning Workshop isolates a basic aspect of playwriting, allowing you to focus on that aspect until you feel you have mastered it. By the end of this workshop, you will have a good sense of the fundamentals of playwriting: creating setting, fleshing out characters, working with conflict, putting together a scenario, and writing a scene.

To best capture the *process* that most experienced playwrights go through when they create a play, the Beginning Workshop encourages you to actively explore and take from the world around you. For instance, you will explore old, familiar places, looking at them as possible settings for plays; you'll observe people you know well and people on the street, thinking about them as possible characters. All your observations will be closely linked to complementary written exercises, where you sit down at your typewriter and turn what you have observed into the various components that make up a play.

Spend no more than a week on each step of the Beginning Workshop, so that you don't lose the continuity of the workshop or get stuck on any one exercise. Work consistently, preferably every day. Find time to do the exercises: Get up a little earlier in the morning. Use your lunch break. Sneak away for an hour after dinner. Be resourceful; you can always make time for yourself to write, even with the most hectic schedule.

And do each step carefully. Some of the steps may seem too simple, too elementary for you, at first. But people who have participated in the Beginning Workshop agree that the more you put into each step of the process, the more you get out. Playwriting is play*building,* learning to put together a play step by step.

Observing the World as a Playwright

Good playwrights are good observers. They spot those little details that say volumes about a person, place, or event. They jot down those sights, sounds, smells, and other sensations we usually miss as we go through our daily lives: the smell of popcorn in a downtown Woolworth's, the sound of bare feet on a polished wooden floor, the movement of seagulls in the air currents behind a commuter ferry. Playwrights borrow constantly from their lives; they ferret away physical sensations and emotional moments they have witnessed or been part of to use in their plays. When writing about—or taking from—an actual experience, a playwright *selects vivid and concrete details* from the experience that best allow an audience to share that experience.

Like warming up before you jog, the first step of the Beginning Workshop has three purposes:

—To help you learn to train your senses to be as open and receptive to the world around you as they were when you were a child.

—To encourage you to start realizing that what you experience (and have experienced) in your life, when observed closely, can be excellent raw material for plays.

—To allow you to begin to describe what you experience (and have experienced) in as succinct and vivid a manner as possible.

All observation and memory is sensory, linked to one or more of the five senses. To capture an audience, you have to appeal to their reality—to what they perceive and what they remember. Ideas, abstract concepts, even emotions, not grounded in the concrete, specific images of everyday life, make for political speeches, not good plays. And, because a play onstage is constantly in motion—characters moving, the action of the play moving forward—only the most vivid, arresting images can communicate to a theater audience. Strong sense stimulation is how a playwright evokes an emotional and intellectual response. The way to an audience's heart and head is through their five senses.

In Marsha Norman's Pulitzer Prize–winning two-character play, *'Night, Mother,* for example, Jessie has to explain to her mother why she is going to commit suicide. All the talk about suicide could easily become abstract and rhetorical, but the playwright is careful to ground the ideas and emotions of the play in accessible, vivid, concrete images. Perhaps the most striking image comes toward the end of the play when Jessie tells her mother that she wouldn't commit suicide if she had *something* worth living for. Not necessarily love. Not achievement. Not even a sense of personal worth. Nothing that grand, high-flown, and rhetorical. If she could wake up in the morning and look forward even to something as simple as rice pudding, that would be enough; she wouldn't commit suicide. When the play was performed on Broadway, the audience laughed a little in recognition, and promptly fell to pieces, understanding Jessie's dilemma completely, devastated by something so real, so tangible, so vivid . . . so effective as rice pudding.

With that in mind, let's try some simple ways of fine-tuning each of the five senses: sight, hearing, touch, smell, and taste:

Sight

Considering sight is our most developed sense, it's amazing how much we *don't* see. Pick two places you go to almost every day. One of the locations should be more public and busy, the other more private and secluded. Both should be places you have learned to take for granted—for example, your kitchen, your office cubicle, a restaurant where you have been eating lunch for years, or a park you walk through every day on your way to work.

Now, just stop and *look* around you for approximately five minutes. Take in all you can *see*. What do you see that you have never seen before? (For example: How long has that billboard for Tastykakes been above Dreyfus' Drugstore? When did Si start replacing his harvest-gold kitchen appliances with almond-colored ones?) How would you describe what you see succinctly and vividly, without using clichés? How does looking closely at either place affect your perception of the place? Look again. What did you miss the first time? Later, away from both locations, try to remember what details you saw. Which details stand out the strongest? Which have you almost forgotten? The next day, go back to the two locations. What did you miss? What did you forget?

Hearing

Pick two places you take for granted, one public and one private, but different from the ones you chose above. Again, just stop, but this time close your eyes for several minutes.

Listen first to the sounds very close to you. Then, thinking in terms of concentric circles, listen to sounds farther and farther away, to the very limit of your hearing "horizon." (Is that a diesel tractor-trailer downshifting way off there on the beltway?) What sounds dominate? What sounds recede? Does this hold true after you have been listening awhile, or has your ear selected other sounds, perhaps more subtle, to focus on? How would you describe what you are hearing in as simple a manner as possible?

Try listening again. What did you miss the first time? What new sounds are there? Later, try to remember what sounds you heard. What sounds are still vivid? Which less so? Have you forgotten some altogether?

Touch

What you are about to do is a lot more challenging than it may seem at first. Have someone place a small everyday object behind your back, so you can't see it. *Feel* its size, its weight, the texture(s) of its surface, any distinctive features or irregularities. Is it hollow? Is it solid? Has it been used? Without the benefit of seeing the object, try to describe the object in minute detail. ("It has a small, worn spot near the . . .") Now, look at the object. Does your description do it justice?

Smell

This sense becomes less sharp as the years go by, but have you noticed that if you smell something with a fragrance just like something from years back, how vividly you remember? A strong whiff of a certain cologne while you're waiting in line for a movie can take you back to the night of your older sister's first date, when she virtually bathed in the same cologne. The smell of the waxy insides of a pint milk carton can transport some people back to their third-grade lunchroom. Using the right sensory details, you, as playwright, can have a similiar effect on your audience.

For this exercise, simply stop and smell various aromas throughout a typical day: your new 100 percent cotton pants, the upholstery in your car, the steps leading down to your subway stop, even your glass of Diet Pepsi. (Does it smell different with or without ice cubes?) Try to describe what you smell both succinctly and with originality.

Taste

Like your sense of smell, taste is a sense that suffers as you grow older, mostly because when we *see* something we assume we know how it'll taste, so we turn off our taste buds. At the risk of sounding like a Weight Watchers' plan, simply slow down as you eat, savoring each bite. Where does the food go in your mouth? How do the texture and taste change as you chew? Is there a distinct aftertaste? How does your sense of taste respond to salt? Sweet? Pungent? Bland? Hot? Cold? Different textures? (To give yourself a real workout, eat an authentic Tex-Mex taco!) Try to describe what you have tasted as objectively and descriptively as possible, without using clichés.

In the following exercise, everything you have been doing with the five senses comes together. But instead of observing directly, you will have the more challenging task of remembering what you observed long ago. Read the biographies of the master playwrights such as Anton Chekhov, Henrik Ibsen, Eugene O'Neill, George Bernard Shaw, and August Strindberg, and you'll see how a playwright's past and present make great raw material for plays. The Beginning Workshop encourages you to realize that *your* life has as much potential to provide raw material for plays as any playwright's—as long as you know how to observe, to remember what you have observed, and to use what you have observed like a playwright. The following exercise is a beginning. At the same time, the exercise actually gives you a little preview of what you'll be doing in the Advanced Workshop, when you'll be delving into your past to find the raw material for your first full-length play.

In the exercise, you'll be recollecting two major events from your past: for example, a wedding, a funeral, leaving someone or someplace you care about, a reunion, a birthday. One event should be pleasant, the other painful. Memory is a very subjective thing, especially when it is shaded with strong positive or negative emotions, so this will be an especially good exercise for training yourself to be as objective and impartial as possible.

For each event you choose, think back; place yourself in the middle of the event. Pretend you're there as an outsider, a detached observer. Using all five senses, try to remember as many *specific sensory details* as possible: the heat of the candles on the birthday cake. How your first communion veil scratched. What Mrs. Cobb's pastry tasted like at the reception after your grandfather's funeral. The pattern of the wallpaper in your parents' living room on the day you left for Vietnam. The possibilities are limitless.

(Note: Despite your efforts to remain objective throughout the exercise, it's very likely that as you remember more and more details, old emotions, old subjective feelings, will return, stronger than ever. It's fine if they do—as long as your descriptions of the sensory details remain as objective as possible.)

When you do the exercise, keep digging for details. Fill in what were probably vague outlines at first. (What were we eating? Were we really eating Campbell's chicken noodle soup right out of the can? What were we drinking? What was that song on the radio? Was it that song by Petula Clark—"Don't Sleep in the Subway"? What game of cards were we playing —Go Fish? Hearts?) Little details give writing life; they give the audience something they can hold on to, something they can relate to.

Sensory Exercise: For each of two major events from your past, make as long a list as you can of all the specific sensory details you can remember. From each list, select eight objective sensory details you feel best recreate the feeling of the event. Write a brief paragraph for each event, arranging the eight details for maximum effect.

Read aloud the two paragraphs you wrote to several people with whom you feel comfortable sharing your work. What is their response? Is it what you hoped it would be? If not, what other details might have better captured the event?

(Note: You may balk at the whole idea of reading anything you have written aloud. Get used to it, because playwriting is "language on its feet." An audience does not have the benefit of the words on a page in front of them to refer back to, to mull over. A play is here, is now, then is gone. Reading your work aloud, hearing—and having others hear—your words spoken is good practice, even on these initial nondialogue exercises.

Also, you may feel shy about sharing your work with anyone else. That's okay for Emily Dickinson writing poetry, not for *you*. Playwriting, more than any other idiom, *is* sharing—*collaborating* with actors, directors, designers and, of course, *performing* the play before an audience. Learning to share your work, learning to deal with criticism, right from the very beginning, will ease you into the spirit of writing for the stage.)

Creating Settings

The physical environment where a playwright places the action of his or her play is called the *setting:* A marriage proposal may be set on the porch outside Aunt Ruth's kitchen, a violent confrontation in the playground in MacArthur Park late at night, a heated argument in the Lathams' powder room, a surreptitious tryst in the Cranberry Room of the Saugatuck Holiday Inn. The importance of the setting is often underrated by new playwrights. Even the simplest setting has a great impact on the action of the play. For instance, an angry shouting match between a man and his seventy-five-year-old father will be very different if the confrontation occurs in the privacy of the man's kitchen or in front of the deli counter at the neighborhood 7-11, right out there for the world to see.

Like all things in theater, even the most "realistic," detailed setting is not reality, but borrows from reality. Experienced playwrights frequently use an actual environment they have observed as the basis for a play's setting (or settings), modifying it to best fit the needs of the play.

Why do experienced playwrights usually base the settings of their plays on real environments? Why don't they just "make up" a setting, depending solely on their imagination? The observations and recollections of an actual environment provide the playwright with many compelling, useful, telling, one-of-a-kind details that even the most fertile imagination could not dream up. For example, composer Stephen Sondheim's incredible game-filled living room inspired the bizarre fun-house setting for Peter Shaffer's *Sleuth*. To create Harry Hope's saloon in *The Iceman Cometh,* Eugene O'Neill combined details from three infamous saloons in lower Manhattan he haunted as a young man. What about environments you know or have known that would make interesting settings for your plays? What about your Great Uncle Kirkman's ramshackle Victorian gazebo as a setting for a romantic interlude? Or the booth with the mechanical fortuneteller at the State Fair your brother once took you to as the backdrop for a couple deciding whether or not to continue their relationship?

When describing a setting, most modern playwrights are as succinct as possible, including in the description only the absolute essentials. Look at the example below.

Sample Setting

A dark studio apartment. There is a worn sofabed and one chair, but no other furniture. In an alcove, there is a sink, a two-burner stove, a rusted under-the-counter refrigerator, a small counter, and shelves above. The single window in the apartment has a folding security gate, closed and locked. A new, inexpensive curtain has been hung over the window. The apartment has three doors: one to the bathroom, one to a closet, and one to the hall outside.

Why such a terse description? Why not discuss the color and pattern of the curtains, whether a half-filled box of Wheaties is lying open on the counter, and so on? Because playwriting is a *collaborative* art. When a play is being produced, the playwright works with a director, actors, and set, costume, and lighting designers. A designer who is told detail for detail how the set is to look, an actor who is told exactly how to play a character, a director who is told how the play should be directed, will feel that their efforts to contribute to the collaborative process are being undermined.

Experienced playwrights know it is best to let the designer "create" the setting of the play. Most designers give the playwright's description of the setting at best a cursory glance and find their inspiration for the setting in the play itself, discovering the setting in the lines the characters speak, the confrontations, and other elements of the play. (For example, a designer reading a play might think to herself, "The Graham boys wrestle in three or four scenes, so I'm going to have to give the setting a large open area. Maybe in front of the sofa. Or over near the bookshelves. . . . The parents seem to be always having cocktails—should I put in a built-in bar? A liquor cabinet? . . . No, wait, there's that scene where Mr. Graham mixes Campari and sodas out on the terrace. Maybe a portable bar would be best then. . . . Yes, because then the Graham boys can slam into it when they wrestle . . .")

In fact, many descriptions of setting you read in published plays are descriptions of the first major production of the play—written *after* the designer(s) created the setting, the lights, and the costumes. Allowing the designer freedom to exercise his or her craft almost always results in a much more satisfying collaboration. When the set is finally constructed, the costumes finished, the furniture and other stage properties in place, and the lights hung, playwrights usually marvel at how much better the designer's interpretation of the setting was than anything the playwright could have come up with alone.

Because you'll ultimately be developing a realistic play in the Advanced Workshop, be especially careful not to demand —or expect—too much detail in production. Especially if your play is produced by a smaller, less-established theater group, fiscal restraints will necessitate some radical, often ingenious, shortcuts. One playwright, for example, included a detailed description of a basement recreation room for a confrontation between two characters. The setting when the play was finally produced? Two Ping-Pong paddles. That's it. The actors mimed playing a vigorous game of Ping-Pong—perfect for physicalizing the confrontation—and the dialogue filled in the rest. In performance, the scene worked wonderfully, it seemed absolutely "realistic." The playwright was stunned.

But a simplified production doesn't mean that you, as playwright, don't need to know *exactly* what the setting should look like. You must know *every* detail in the setting in order to use the setting to its maximum effect. Edward Albee's two-character play, *The Zoo Story,* which takes place in Central Park, is usually produced with just a park bench. But having the characters talk about what they see and have seen that day evokes Central Park beautifully, in all its somewhat glorious, somewhat decrepit detail. When you read or see a performance of *The Zoo Story,* you know that before the playwright sat down to write, he knew his setting inside out, using every detail to its maximum effect.

Basing your setting on actual environments you observe or

remember makes exploring and working with settings much easier and much more fruitful. This step of the Beginning Workshop allows you to practice creating stage settings from actual environments. It builds on the work you did with observing and remembering. It encourages you to look closely and objectively at familiar and foreign environments, both present and past, then to be able to distill the details you remember into as succinct a description as possible, ready for later use as a stage setting.

> *Exploration Exercise:* Explore several environments, at least one public and one private. Also try to find one environment that is unfamilar to you. Concentrate on the physical setting; filter out any people or activities. Using all five senses, jot down as many details as possible.

Think about how you respond to the environment. How does it make you feel? Happy? Sad? Indifferent? Nervous? Tranquil? What sensory details in the environment do you think make you feel that way? (The hand-printed signs in a diner that consistently misspell the word "fried." Faintly hearing the television in one of the bedrooms upstairs. The smell of stale tobacco as you enter Mr. Winter's office.) Would someone else respond the same as you? For instance, would your best friend respond the same way as you to a well-manicured garden? Or a clean but cluttered kitchen? Or an indoor shopping mall? Why?

How does the environment reflect the person or persons who created it? Or the person or persons who use it? (A bathroom with a sunken marble tub or a Jacuzzi in a house that is otherwise fairly modest. Or Van Gogh's "Sunflowers," done in crewel, above the sofa.) Does the environment try to appeal to a certain kind of person? (Compare the sensory details in a high-tech singles' bar and those in a neighborhood bar that, except for adding a Space Invaders game, hasn't changed its decor since the mid-1950s.) Use objective, concrete details you have observed to back up your guesses.

Then, just for fun, think about how you might put that environment onstage. What details would you emphasize? What changes, drastic and small, might have to be made to make the environment work as a stage setting? What kinds of scenes would you put in the setting? An intimate moment? A political rally? A chance meeting? A domestic quarrel?

In the following exercise, you'll be creating two settings from two similar environments, one environment in the present that you can observe in detail, the other from your past —someplace you no longer see, someplace with which you have some sort of emotional connection. The two environments can be, for example, your present kitchen and your Aunt Rosa's kitchen. Or a park near your home and the park where you walked all the time when you were taking night classes in accounting and in love for the second time. Don't worry whether or not the environments are "theatrical" enough. Do, however, enjoy working with the environments you choose; the settings you "create" at the end of the exercise will be used for scenes you write later in the workshop.

When doing the exercise, observe and remember as many sensory details as you can. Be especially careful not to stint on details from the past environment. Because the two environments are similar, use your observations of the present environment to cue your memory of the past environment. (For example, if you choose two kitchens, first describe the present refrigerator, then try to remember the past refrigerator—or ice box!—using the present refrigerator as a model: How did the door(s) open? What were the shelves like? What smells did it have? Did the inside light work? What kind of pitcher was the orange juice kept in?)

Remember to remain objective. Be especially careful of any heavy-duty emotional shading. (For example, don't say, "the *magical* aroma of her chocolate chip cookies"; say instead "the aroma of her chocolate chip cookies.") Learn early that, as a playwright, you have the responsibility of allowing *both* your collaborators and your audience freedom to use their imaginations. If anything, encourage your collaborators and especially your audience to *work*—to think for themselves. You'll hold their attention better. And, ultimately you'll be much, much happier with the results.

(Note: Don't ever let yourself think that an environment is impossible to recreate onstage. Sometimes radical and imaginative surgery on the actual environment may be necessary. But that's what writing is all about, right? For example, here is what happened in a recent workshop:

A woman was writing a scene about the end of a close friendship between herself and two other women that occurred while they were climbing the sheer face of a cliff in Estes Park, Colorado. Thinking of the setting literally, the playwright felt the conflict would only work as a film until she came up with this ingenious solution: She placed the entire action of the scene on a narrow ledge, halfway up the climb. In production, a bare stage, with the actors imagining the perimeter of the ledge, was all that was necessary to create a breaktakingly exciting situation—and it was a terrific setting for creating conflict; no one could just walk away!)

> *Setting Exercise:* For a present environment you observe and a similar past environment you remember, make two lists as long as you can of all the specific sensory details in each environment. From the lists, write two short, pithy descriptions, one for each "setting."

Read the descriptions of the two settings aloud to several people whose opinions you trust. How do they respond to the environments you're describing? Do they respond differently from what you expected? Do they respond differently from each other? Why?

Building Characters

Creating vivid, three-dimensional characters with a life of their own is probably the greatest challenge a new playwright faces. Yet many potential "characters" exist in the world around you—in relatives, friends, acquaintances, and others you have known. If you read the biographies, letters, journals, and notebooks of master playwrights such as Chekhov, Ibsen, O'Neill, Shaw, and Strindberg, you'll see time and time again how often they used people they knew as models for their characters. Even the most ordinary person can be the beginnings of an extraordinary character onstage.

When describing a character, just as when describing a setting, most modern playwrights are as succinct as possible. The following information usually is included:

—The name of the character
—The character's age
—A brief physical description
—The relationship of the character to other characters in the play.

A few hints when putting together a character description:

—Choose the name carefully; a name often says a lot about the character. (A Rose is not a Rosa is not a Rosie . . .) When basing the character on a real person, consider a name other than the name of the actual person; it'll allow you a greater degree of objectivity.

—If you make too detailed a physical description of the character, most likely it will be ignored. If you insist that the character be tall, blond, and blue-eyed, the odds are the actor perfect for the role will be short, dark-haired, and have hazel eyes. Unless critical to the role (such as a young man with a serious weight problem), physical description should be kept to a minimum. (A perfect example of why: Two actors have dazzled Broadway audiences playing the character of Willy Loman in Arthur Miller's *Death of a Salesman:* Lee J. Cobb in the original 1947 production, a large man in all respects, slow-moving, and with a deep, gravelly voice; and Dustin Hoffman, in the 1984 revival, short, wiry, a man with certain physical tension, a higher-pitched voice. Physically, the two actors are night and day, but the playwright thought both did absolute justice to the role.)

—Comments on the personality of the character should be kept to a minimum. Remember: The character description is for an actor, not a reader. Any good actor learns who his or her character is by exploring the play, from reading the lines and reading between the lines, not by reading the playwright's suggestion about how to play the character.

The character descriptions of all the major characters in the play are usually grouped together with a description of the setting and time of the action on a separate page before the play itself (although some playwrights describe the major characters when the character first enters). See the example below.

Sample Character Description

Steve Watson, Grace's brother-in-law, is confined to a wheelchair, having lost the use of his legs in a freak accident at a ROTC summer training camp. He is twenty-nine, strong, good-looking, tries to be as optimistic as possible, but a slight bitter edge keeps surfacing.

This is brief and to the point; an effective outline for the actor to fill in. Some modern playwrights sometimes include a little more detail. But, interestingly enough, many modern playwrights provide no character descriptions at all, believing—quite correctly—the actor portraying the character will find out all he or she needs to know about the character from reading and rehearsing the play itself, and that by exploring the character, *the actor ultimately will play the character better than if he or she is told how the character is to be played.*

Rule of thumb: Include only the absolute essentials when putting together a character description.

But that does not mean that you, as playwright, are not responsible for knowing your characters inside out. A fully rounded understanding of *who your characters are* is essential to the success of your play. That's why experienced playwrights almost always base their characters on people they know and have known: Using a real person as a model provides facets of character and insights into human nature that just would not be available if the playwright depended solely on his or her imagination.

A simple, but very revealing, aspect of personality is how people *dress*—what they wear and how they wear it. Building on your work with observation and memory, look closely at such aspects of dress as clothing (style, material, color, combinations, age and condition of the clothing, even brand name), jewelry (and other ornamentation), footwear, hairstyle, grooming, colognes or perfumes, eyeglasses (or contacts)—the possibilities are limitless. And just as important as what the person wears is how the person wears it. (Does his expensive sweater hang off his shoulders? And is it buttoned all wrong? Does she constantly twist her diamond ring? Is his right sneaker always untied? Does she chew on her glasses more than she wears them? Is he continuously touching his hair even though every hair is in place?)

When observing people, try to suppress your tendency to be subjective and judgmental. You might, for example, want to jot down, "He was wearing an old white silk Nehru jacket that was somewhat worn around the cuff of the left sleeve." Not

"He looked stupid wearing that kind of jacket. Doesn't he know Nehrus went out years ago?"

To begin, observe several people—at least one you should know intimately, one should be an acquaintance, and one should be a total stranger. Remember as many details as you can about what the people wear and how they wear it. (Note: When observing strangers, make an effort not to overhear them talking. Limit yourself to how they dress—that's the challenge of this step of the workshop.) Later, when you're by yourself, jot down a list of things you remember. Then, looking at the list, consider first the people you know fairly well —relatives, friends, and acquaintances. Think about whether what you have observed about each person's dress reflects what you know about the person.

Now, think about the strangers you have observed. Exercise your imagination by making up little personality profiles/ life histories for them, based on what they wear and how they wear it: Where do they live? What kind of car do they drive? (Do they drive at all?) What are their favorite foods? What is their favorite section of the newspaper? Do they like to dance? Would they excel at Trivial Pursuit? Do they collect ceramic owls? Do they play miniature golf? Do they fall in love with older women? Give your imagination free rein, but always back up everything you guess about the people with specific details you have observed about their dress. ("She was wearing stiletto heels from the fifties, but she kept falling against her friend, laughing. Therefore, I think she . . .")

In the following exercise, you will begin to build two characters from two people you have observed or remembered. The first person you will be working with should be a total stranger, someone you observe from a distance—at a coffee shop, in a park, or in some other busy public place where you will not be conspicuous. The second person should be someone you remember, someone you have had some sort of significant emotional relationship with—a family member, a close friend, a romance—but it must be someone you haven't seen for a long time.

When doing the exercise, begin with the stranger, whom we'll call the "present character." Make a list of all the details you observe about what the present character is wearing and how he or she wears it. Then, using that list as a guide, jot down all the details you recall about what the "past character" wore and how the person wore it. (Try to remember the past character on one specific day, in one specific outfit. It's a challenge, but it's possible to do; use the memory of one detail to trigger the memory of another. ["Her shoes were those black patent leather Mary Janes with . . . silver, no, brass buckles . . . and she had . . . that's right, white anklets embroidered with some sort of little flowers, um . . . Violets? No, roses. They were pink, that's right."])

From the lists, you'll be putting together a brief paragraph about how the present character and past character dress. When writing the paragraph, select only the most vivid and revealing details. Be careful not to embellish; be as objective as possible. Reread and cut any excess, especially any emotional shading.

Character Exercise: Write a short, pithy paragraph about how a present stranger you observe (the "present character") and a person you were close to that you haven't seen for some time (the "past character") dress. Then, based on your observations and recollections, write a brief personality profile/life history for both the "present character" and the "past character."

Read your descriptions of the "characters" and their personality profiles/life histories aloud to several people. How do they respond? Why?

Putting Your Characters in a Setting

You have taken the first steps toward creating two characters; now you can begin fleshing out the characters, making them more fully dimensional, more stageworthy. Characters onstage are revealed by what they *do* and what they *say*. Many new playwrights depend totally on dialogue to create characters; they "see" their characters only as bodiless voices, not as people in an environment, physically relating to the environment and the other characters in it. New playwrights often don't realize that what environment the character is in and what the character does in that environment has a major impact on the dialogue.

A playwright has to be aware of everything his or her character is doing in a setting—the relative position of the characters to other characters in the setting, where the character moves, how the character moves, what the character touches, picks up, puts down, plays with. Think of a seduction scene between two characters, set in a parlor. Whether the character being seduced chooses to sit on the sofa or in the chair or remains standing affects the dynamics—even the outcome—of the scene!

The character's activities in a setting are called *business*. Experienced playwrights often indicate the subtle, confusing, and particularly important business in their play by inserting non-dialogue *stage directions* in the dialogue (more on stage directions and their use later in the Beginning Workshop). Once again, most experienced playwrights try to keep their stage directions to an absolute minimum for the same reason they keep their descriptions of the characters and the setting short—to encourage *collaboration*. Competent directors and actors, allowed to explore the play in rehearsal, often devise much more interesting, original business than if the playwright dictates what the business should be. (Fact of life: Suggest a piece of business in a play and the director and actors usually will try their damnedest *not* to do what you tell them—just to prove they can be as imaginative as you.)

Once again, just because you don't write it down, doesn't mean that you don't have to know in detail what each one of your characters is doing in the setting. Are the characters close together? Sitting? Standing? Is one character paging through a magazine or in rapt attention as the other character talks? Are the characters in a public or private place? The questions you can ask are limitless.

What *specific* activities might the characters do in a specific setting? What is there in the setting for the characters to play around with? Two characters, a man and a woman, in Roxie's Beauty Parlor after hours, for example: Would the woman tease her hair while she talks? Or constantly glance at the mirrors for some sort of reassurance? Because he was bored, would the man swivel in one of the chairs? Or play with one of the hand-held hair dryers? Or open bottles of dye, maybe even spilling henna rinse on himself—and yell at the woman because of it? Would the woman pick up a tuft of cut hair from the floor and say it reminds her of someone she once knew (unconsciously making the man jealous)? Again, the possibilities are limitless.

The best way to increase your awareness of what a character might do in a setting is to observe real people in actual environments. Watching people *do* such seemingly unimportant things as eating lunch in a diner, combing their hair in the reflection of a store window, or reading the newspaper on the bus, gives you invaluable glimpses into who those people are, sharpening your powers of observation and insight, and providing a gold mine of character details for future use.

A little on-your-feet work first. Observe several people—at least one should be someone you know well, one should be an acquaintance, and one should be a total stranger—as they perform everyday activities. These activities can be work-oriented, domestic, or recreational. They might include: washing dishes, opening doors, dancing, trying to figure out how to use a new VCR, putting on socks, reading the newspaper on a crowded bus, playing rugby (or watching rugby), playing

Space Invaders, typing the ninth draft of a business letter—absolutely anything.

Suppose, for example, you choose to observe people eating a sandwich. You might consider the following: Do they use both hands to eat the sandwich? Before eating, do they cut the sandwich in half? In quarters? Do they tear off pieces as they eat? Or do they hold the sandwich near their face, staring absently at the sandwich as they chew? Do they eat quickly? Slowly? Do they talk while they eat? Do they read? Do they lift up the bread to look at the filling before eating? Do they take the sandwich apart and just pick at the filling? Do they leave crusts or corners? If some of the filling drops out as the person is eating, do they immediately put it back in their sandwich? With a fork? With their fingers? Or do they just leave it lying on their plate? On their lap? Do they wipe their fingers frequently? On a napkin? On their clothes?

You can ask question after question, and each reveals a little more about the person you're observing. (Chances are, in fact, as you read through the list of questions above, you visualized a number of different people, not just one, eating a sandwich depending on what was being done with the sandwich. A person who cuts his or her sandwich in quarters is not usually the same person who leaves dropped filling lying on his or her lap. But then again . . .)

Jot down your observations—either as you're observing or, if the circumstances don't allow your bringing out your notebook and pencil, then later, when you have a moment to yourself. Again, when writing down your observations, try to be as objective, precise, and succinct as possible. ("He didn't seem to notice that the deviled ham was dropping onto his lap," is a lot more revealing than, "The guy was a total slob.") What do you think the activity reveals about the person? Be careful to back up your subjective appraisals with details you have observed. Compare two or more people doing the same activity. What are the similarities? The obvious differences? The subtle differences? If possible, share your observations and insights with other people. Do they agree with your insights? Why?

In the following exercise, you'll need the "present character" and the "past character" you created in the last exercise. And you'll need the present and past "settings" you worked on in "Creating Settings." The following exercise will provide you with the chance to test your imagination and ingenuity as you combine the settings and the characters to take your first steps toward both character development and building a dramatic situation.

You'll begin the exercise by placing your *present* character in your *past* setting. You'll have the character do a simple, specific piece of business with some part of the setting that reveals something about who the character is and why the character is in the past setting. For example, if the present character is a young girl and your past setting is a park, you might have her cheat at hopscotch. Put an older man on a diet in a kitchen late at night and he might just stand for several seconds in front of an open refrigerator door, close it, then open it again.

"Oh, no," you're probably saying. "My present character is a 6 foot 3 inch garage mechanic, covered with grease, and my past setting is the frilly white bedroom my niece had when she was four!" Good! Contrasts like that make the exercise all the more interesting. *Don't* throw out either the character or the setting in order to make the exercise easier. The challenge of the remaining exercises in the Beginning Workshop is working with—and making the most of—what you have, constantly stretching your creativity.

Of course, you'll have to make choices about the relationship of the present character and the past setting. You'll have to invent a little piece here and there. For instance, why is the character in the setting? Is the environment foreign or familiar to the character? What year is it? (The past? The present? Some time in-between?) What season is it? What time of day? Why is the character performing the specific piece of business he or she is performing?

When doing the exercise, take what you know (or invented) about the character and the setting, and using a little ingenuity, create the *circumstances* that would allow what the character is doing in the environment to make perfect sense. Explore all the possibilities. Make the situation work, no matter how far-fetched it seems at first. Find the perfect piece of business for the character to do in the environment.

For example, a woman in one workshop actually found herself with a 6 foot 3 inch garage mechanic for her present character and a frilly white girl's bedroom for her past environment. But she invented the *circumstances* which permitted an activity that was not only believable but also touching, revealing, and compelling.

The woman decided that the garage mechanic was in his daughter's bedroom while the daughter was away. The mechanic simply picked up one of his daughter's favorite dolls from the floor and put it on the bed. But the woman's description of the piece of business—the love of the mechanic, his fear of getting the doll dirty, his clumsiness—made for a poignant, Chaplinesque moment.

When doing the exercise, think of the piece of business being performed in front of an audience by an actor. The piece of business should be simple, focused, and revealing. Think in terms of bold strokes. Complex, unnecessarily complicated activities become muddy onstage, hard to "read" from twenty rows back.

When describing the present character's piece of business, be succinct and objective. Read the description, then ask yourself, "Is this a piece of business that will make someone say, 'Yes, I *know* that character!' " If not, continue searching for a more vivid and revealing piece of business. Think of all the objects in the environment. Think of all the quirks in the character. Explore all the possibilities.

Characters in a Setting Exercise: Place the "present character" in the "past setting." Have the character perform a simple, specific piece of business with some part of the setting that reveals something about both who the character is and why the character is in the environment. Describe the activity in a short, pithy paragraph. Repeat the exercise, describing the "past character" performing a piece of business in the "present setting."

When you have completed both descriptions, share them with several people. Do they feel the piece of business you chose succinctly and vividly captures both the character and the reason for the character being in the setting? Why?

Your Characters Talk

Now that you have a solid understanding of your two characters—their histories, their personalities, how they respond to certain environments, how they interact with a setting—you're ready to have them talk. Onstage, a character talking is called *dialogue*. How a character talks is central to the success of a play. Yet it's often a stumbling block for new playwrights, who tend to make all their characters talk alike—usually just like the playwright!

Experienced playwrights know character is revealed not only by *what* the character says but, more important, by *how* that particular character says it. There are two important aspects of dialogue that help to differentiate how characters speak:

—*Vocabulary:* What kinds of words and phrases the character might use. (Compare, for example, the vocabulary of an ex–flower child from Santa Cruz who's now heading a chain of profitable organic bakeries called "One Smart

Cookie" with a second-generation dockworker born and bred in Joliet, Illinois.)

—*Vocal Pattern:* The idiosyncracies of the character's speech. (Does each of her sentences end with a question mark? When does he pause? Does he mumble? Ramble? Speak succinctly and to the point? What words or phrases does she emphasize? Or repeat?)

Experienced playwrights often "collect" interesting vocabulary and vocal patterns. Pulitzer Prize–winning playwright David Mamet has file drawers crammed with snatches of conversations he overheard while riding on buses, working at his many part-time jobs, passing people on the street, eating in restaurants—wherever he went.

How do you develop a good ear for dialogue? Eavesdrop. Constantly. Shamelessly. Eavesdrop on friends talking, acquaintances discussing, strangers arguing, every conversation you can overhear. But eavesdrop in a very special way.

As you listen to people talk, focus first on *what* people are saying—the content of their conversation. Listen to what facts they are telling, what points they are bringing up, what stories they are sharing, and so on. Then focus on *how* people are talking. Listen for *vocabulary*. Jot down—or remember to jot down later—distinctive words and phrases, and how they're used.

Then focus on *vocal patterns*:

—*Rhythms:* Does the person's voice sound sing-song? Forceful? Hesitant? Sometimes forceful, sometimes hesitant?

—*Emphasis:* Does the person emphasize the beginnings of sentences? The ends? Particular words?

—*Pauses:* Does the person pause frequently? Infrequently? After sentences? In the middle of sentences? After particular phrases?

Does the person seem to think before speaking? Does the person talk nonstop? In half-sentences? Monosyllables? Grunts? Does the person speak at the same time as other people? Is the person articulate or a mumbler? Do the ends of sentences tend to drop off? What is the *tone of voice* of the person talking? Is it soothing? Bored? Passionate? Does the person whine? The observations you can make are virtually limitless, and each insight reveals a little more about the person talking.

When you have a chance, jot down as much as you can about what you have observed. What are the people revealing about themselves, both consciously and unconsciously, as they talk? When listening to people you know well, think about how their speech reflects their personalities. When overhearing strangers, invent personality profiles/life histories for these people, as you did in "Building Characters." Remember to back up your appraisals with specifics you have observed. (For example, you might jot down, "He's a natural storyteller, who speaks with a lot of gusto, until he starts to talk about his former wife—which he seems to do quite often. Then his voice drops and he becomes hesitant, even though he speaks highly of her. Therefore, I think he feels . . .")

Up to now, you have been encouraged to approach the exercises with as much objectivity as possible. Well, here's your revenge: The following exercise is pure, unadulterated subjectivity—with a catch. You allow your two characters to be as subjective, emotional, and biased as *they* want!

Begin by building upon what you have learned about your two characters from your work in the previous exercises. (At this point, you should no longer be thinking of them as the "past character" and the "present character," but simply two *characters*.

Chances are, in fact, that the two characters have already begun to evolve a "life" of their own, quite separate from the real people they're based on. That's wonderful. That's what writing is all about.)

Before you begin working on the exercise, think about who these two characters are. Exercise your imagination: Invent some sort of relationship between the two. They might be family members, old friends, new friends, or practically strangers. Invent a brief history of their relationship, making up specific and concrete details about the events, places, and people they share in common. Just make sure the basic personalities of the characters remain consistent with what you have learned from the previous exercises. Also, to make the exercise as interesting and *dramatic* as possible, try to imagine the relationship of the two characters as being essentially antagonistic.

In the exercise, you will be writing a brief *monologue* for each character. A monologue is an aspect of dialogue in which someone talks without being interrupted; in the theater, a monologue is sometimes said to another character, or directly to the audience. Later in the Beginning Workshop, you'll learn more about the proper form for typing out a script of a play but, for the purposes of the exercise, below is a model that shows how to type out a monologue. (You should type all your work—notes, drafts, final versions, everything. It's amazing how much more objectively you can view your writing when it is neatly typed, as opposed to handwritten. You might as well get in practice; when you submit a play to theaters and contests, the play *has* to be typed.)

Sample Monologue

HARRIET

There was this girl—my best friend, I guess, but okay, how many best friends do you have when you're that age? Patti Tarbell: the kind of girl who's too much everything you wish you were but are probably glad you're not. But you'd never admit that to yourself. The kind of girl, when you're walking next to her, no matter how old you are, you feel like you're wearing braces. On your legs. It's true. And

Patti Tarbell knew it. That's why she chose me to be her best friend, I made just a wonderful contrast . . .

Note that the name is centered and in capital letters, and the monologue itself is in a block, directly below the name, running margin to margin. (Standard margins are 1¼ inch top and bottom, 1½ inch left, 1 inch right.) That's all you really need to know for now.

In the two monologues you'll be writing for the exercise, the characters will be:

—Describing each other

—Giving their *point of view* about the relationship of the two.

Pretend each character is talking directly to someone who is a relatively sympathetic—but not *too* sympathetic—listener. In the monologue, the character speaking should try to persuade the person listening to feel the same way he or she feels about both the other character and the relationship as a whole. Let the characters be as subjective as they like about each other and the relationship. Hostilities, affection, prejudices, and other emotional responses can come right to the surface. (For example: "He's an absolute creep!" Or "It was sweet, wasn't it, him coming all the way to pick me up when the hose busted on the Oldsmobile." Or "I think she's worn that same dress since I first knew her." Or even such eloquent expressions as "Yeah? Baloney!") Let each of your characters have a field day, but remember that you, as playwright, should try to remain as objective as possible.

And remember: The characters want to win their listener over to their point of view, so probably they'll try to share their point of view in the most interesting way possible: *by telling a story,* with a coherent narrative thread, a bit of suspense, possibly some sort of payoff—all the elements of good storytelling (and good playwriting). (Of course, if either character is not a natural storyteller, then the character might be-revealed by how *badly* he or she tries to win the listener over.)

The trick to the exercise is that as the characters speak, *they should be revealing more about themselves* than the character (or relationship) they are describing. This happens, of course, not because of *what* the character says, but *how* the character says it—namely, vocabulary and vocal pattern. So you have to let the characters "speak for themselves," with all the quirks and idiosyncracies that say, "This is who I am. This is how I see the world."

Monologue Exercise: Invent some sort of antagonistic relationship for the two characters you have been working with since "Building a Character." For each character, write a 3-minute (about a single-spaced typed page) monologue, addressed to the audience. The characters should describe each other, and give their point of view of the relationship of the two characters.

After completing the two monologues, reread them. Cut any excess, especially anything that does not seem true to the character speaking. If possible, "cast" the two monologues: Have two friends who remind you of the characters read the monologues aloud. Have other friends listen. Does each character's speech seem natural? Or forced? Have you vividly captured the characters? Their vocabulary? Their vocal patterns? Their personality? Their point of view? If not, it might be a good idea to spend time on "Creating Characters" and "Putting Your Characters in a Setting" in order to learn more about *who* your characters are.

Putting Together a Basic Scenario

Now you'll be turning what you have been working with into a short scene. A *scene* is a subdivision of a play in which the setting is fixed and the time continuous; it's the basic building block of playwriting. Think of a scene as a microplay; a successful scene contains all the elements of good playwriting *in miniature.* If you can write good scenes, and learn to link them together into a compelling story, writing a play becomes cake—layer cake.

In this final phase of the Beginning Workshop, you will learn the process of scene building. You turn what you have been working with in the workshop up to this point into a short scene—in *two* steps:

1. By putting together a basic scenario—essentially a narrative outline of the play, telling the *story* of the play or scene.
2. By writing the actual scene itself, complete with dialogue and stage directions.

A scenario is the bane of many a new playwright, who just wants to plunge right in and write dialogue. But what new playwrights forget is that a successful scene—and, by extension, a successful play—is a *story.* A play is a story as much as any work of fiction is a story. A story is a series of interconnected incidents, moving forward from beginning to middle to end. The engine of the story, the element of the story that propels the play forward, is *conflict.*

At the heart of every successul scene—and, by extension, every successful play—lies a strong sense of *conflict.* Conflict has many shades of meaning: struggle, clash, battle, controversy, disagreement, opposition, collision, fight. Onstage, conflict can be as bold as a rumble between two rival gangs or as subtle as two old friends bantering over who picks up the tab for lunch. Conflict propels the story forward, maintaining interest, pulling the audience along—often simply by making the audience wonder *who will win out, which side of the conflict will prevail.* Following the story is following the conflict. New playwrights usually have a hard time realizing that without a strong, clear-cut conflict, a scene—and, by extension, a play—is only so much aimless talk, and an audience soon loses interest.

For our purposes, let's say that conflict is: A character *wants* something that someone (or something) tries to *prevent* that character from getting. What the character wants might be a person (to have Louise marry him), an object (to gain control of the family inheritance), a place (to go to New York to begin a new career), or an idea (to find happiness or security). Four words to remember when thinking about conflict are: *goal, motivation, obstacles(s),* and *tactics*. To round out the definition of conflict then:

> A character wants *(motivation)* something *(goal)* but someone (or something) tries to prevent *(obstacles)* the character from achieving his or her goal. If the character's motivation is strong enough, the character will try various means of overcoming the obstacle(s) *(tactics)* to achieve his or her *goal*.

That, in a nutshell, is conflict.

For example, in the following synopsis, consider the elements of conflict in Lanford Wilson's two-character play, *Talley's Folly*.

> The play takes place on a July evening in 1944. Matt, a 42-year-old accountant, has come down from St. Louis to the small town of Lebanon, Missouri, with a specific *goal:* to convince Sally, a 31-year-old nursing aide, to marry him. His *motivation,* his love for Sally, is strong. In the year since their very brief romance the summer before, he has written to her continuously. (She wrote a note back once, to tell him to stop writing.) He has tried to visit her at the hospital where she works. (Each time, she hid from him.) On the day the play takes place, Matt, out of loneliness and his love for Sally, has walked out on an important assignment in St. Louis, driven straight through to Lebanon, and even confronted Sally's gun-toting brother, in his effort to find her.
>
> But the biggest *obstacle* Matt faces is Sally herself. A

strong-willed, self-protective woman, resigned to being a spinster, Sally will not even admit to herself that she loves Matt. She tells Matt in no uncertain terms to leave her alone, to drive right back to St. Louis that night. To win her, to overcome the emotional *obstacles* between them, Matt tries the following *tactics:* Being playful. Trying to make Sally remember their brief romance the summer before. Appealing to her loneliness, her fear of becoming a spinster. He even points out that she's wearing a new dress, just to chase him off her family's property. Several times, Matt physically restrains Sally from leaving the boathouse where they meet. Ultimately, he goads her into a direct head-to-head confrontation.

Finally, late in the play, Matt presses Sally to confront the real reason behind her being terrified of falling in love with him. And two lonely people come together in the night, the *conflict* resolved.

It's a difficult step taking your raw material—characters, relationships, setting—and putting it all together into a cohesive, compelling story. This is where a scenario proves invaluable. Experienced playwrights use a scenario to map out the conflict. Written as a narrative (rather than as dialogue), your scenario will force you to look at your scene as a story. Any flaws in the story are much more apparent, not hidden by sparkling, but essentially purposeless and/or directionless, dialogue.

A playwright has to have a thorough knowledge of what he or she is writing about. Throughout the Beginning Workshop, you have been learning to lay the groundwork for a scene and, by extension, a play. Exploring your raw material, understanding your raw material, what can and cannot be done with it, is the whole foundation of what you're writing. The more thorough your exploration, the richer the final product will be. Many inexperienced playwrights, eager for results, skip over the groundwork and plunge right into writing dialogue. The results are usually flat dialogue, uninteresting characters, and conflicts that go nowhere. Many experienced playwrights spend a year or more exploring a full-length play—taking notes, doing research, making observations, reviewing the raw material, creating scenarios, building a solid foundation for the actual playwriting. Putting together basic scenarios for the scenes you'll be doing in the Beginning and Intermediate Workshops will allow you to strengthen your skills at scenario-making before you attack a full-length play. So, do not skimp on the scenario. Many participants in workshops have said, "I just want to write a play." Putting together a good scenario for a scene is an important step in writing a play. Playwriting is play*building*. Give the scenario time and attention.

In the exercise that follows, you'll take the two characters you have been working with. Place them in the present setting from "Creating Settings." Maintain the relationship—especially the antagonism—between the characters you developed in "Your Characters Talk."

Invent a conflict situation in which one of the two characters *wants* something very much and the other character tries his or her best to *prevent* the first character from achieving this goal. Make sure that what the first character wants is specific, whether it's an object, person, place, or idea. For example, the first character might want to have the other character—his girlfriend for the past seven years—meet his ex-wife who's in from Tulsa. Or the first character might want to leave her job at IBM in Atlanta—a job that supports both her and the other character—to try to become a potter in New Mexico. The possibilities are limitless.

In the exercise, you'll be writing the scenario for a brief scene in which the first character has enough *motivation* to make a real effort to achieve his or her *goal,* whereas the other character, equally motivated, creates every *obstacle* he or she can to prevent that goal from being achieved. Both characters use whatever *tactics* the situation allows. The goal, motivations, obstacles, and tactics should be consistent with what you know about the characters, their relationship, the setting, the time period, and any other elements you have been developing throughout the workshop.

When working through the scenario for this scene, use all the resources you have at your disposal. Go back to the groundwork you laid in the previous steps of the workshop to find tactics and obstacles. For example, *setting:* Is there a door to slam? A Tequila Sunrise to throw in his face? Or *language:* Would he shout to get his way? Or be silent? Or whine? Or swear? Or *physical activities:* Would he rip up the only copy of her manuscript? Would she just go on playing the guitar and ignore him? Or the *personality profile/life history* of the character: Would he lie through his teeth? Would she bring up something he'd done in the past?

Make the story *compelling*—make the audience want to follow the struggle of these two characters, how their conflict develops, and how and if it's resolved. Make the conflict as *exciting* as possible, without destroying the "reality" of the scene. Once you have decided what the conflict is, don't settle for obvious or trite tactics and obstacles. Explore; find tactics and obstacles that would make an audience sit up and say, "Yes! That really captures the conflict! Good! I know that character; I see that relationship! Hey, isn't it clever what the playwright did with . . ."

When writing the scenario, describe everything that happens in the scene from the lights up to lights down. But *use no dialogue*. Think in terms of *action*. Describe the action with flair, vigor, enthusiasm, and élan, like a good sports announcer would (an *objective* sports announcer, not a Howard Cosell). For example:

> Josh comes in from the garden and tells Lena to pack her things, they're leaving for Denver right now. Lena tells him to wash up for dinner. (She's not taking him seriously; he's said this a thousand times.) Josh cuts her off as she heads for the refrigerator, telling her that this time he's serious.

Lena opens the refrigerator and asks Josh if he wants a Molson or Gatorade with dinner. . . .

Working through the scene in this manner will provide a sound framework for the dialogue to come. It allows you to figure out the motivations, goals, tactics, and obstacles beyou write a line of dialogue. Successful dialogue has so much going on *beneath* the dialogue. A good scenario helps you decide and *use* what's going on in the scene.

Scenario Exercise: As the foundation for a short scene, put together a basic scenario—a narrative description of everything that happens in the scene from lights up to lights down.

After you have sketched out the narrative description of the scene, look it over carefully. Can any of the motivations, goals, tactics, or obstacles be made more clear? More precise? Does the scene stray? Does it just seem to lie flat in spots? Any long, arid stretches where "nothing happens"? Are the relationships consistent? Interesting? Honest? Does the "story" move forward? Modify, replace, or delete any dead weight where the conflict lags.

Writing a Scene—the Basic Building Block of Playwriting

Turning the scenario you created in the last exercise into a short scene is the last step of the Beginning Workshop. By developing characters and a setting from life, inventing a conflict situation, putting together a scenario, and finally writing a short scene, you'll have gone through the same process an experienced playwright goes through to create a play—*in miniature*. If you can write an effective scene, you'll have little difficulty writing a play. Any play, when taken apart, is a string of interconnected, discrete scenes.

Because the following exercise is a scene, complete with dialogue and characters interacting in a setting, now is a perfect time to learn the preferred form for putting together the *script* for a play. A script is the acting version of a play, used by directors and actors in rehearsal. It differs from the published version of the play.

When submitting a script, always type it, either in pica or elite (preferably pica), on good 16- or 20-pound bond paper. Allow ample margins, for binding and for the directors and actors to jot down notes. The standard format for margins is: top and bottom 1¼ inch; left 1½ inch; right 1 inch.

On a separate page preceding the play proper, put the descriptions of characters, the description of setting, the time of year, the time of day together in the following manner:

Sample Style Sheet for Characters, Time, and Setting

Characters:

HARRIET is twenty-six. STEPHEN's friend. Still looks at herself as an ungainly, overweight teenager. Dressed for a night on the town.

BRIAN is twenty-eight. STEPHEN's other friend. Self-styled eccentric. Wears a tuxedo, circa 1910, and hightop sneakers.

Time:

Late September. Early evening.

Setting:

A construction site in downtown Minneapolis.

The format for typing the script of a play varies slightly from playwright to playwright. Below is a fairly standard model for writing dialogue and stage directions.

(Note: When trying to determine how long your play will run, allow approximately 1 minute running time for each page of script.)

Sample Style Sheet for Play Scripts

(BRIAN is playing an old, red, toy piano. HARRIET sits a little away, huddled against the cold, an elaborate tropical drink at her side.)

HARRIET

It's just lousy; it's freezing out and sitting—

BRIAN

(As he plays)

Harry, what do you expect, it's October—

HARRIET

September twenty-seventh. September isn't cold; it shouldn't be. And having drinks out in the middle of a lot construction debris, it's a lousy place to celebrate Stephen's birthday. Especially since Stephen canceled out on us at the last minute. It's just very lousy. (On the verge of tears) And I'm feeling very sorry for myself.

BRIAN

And reveling in it.

HARRIET

Very much. But don't let me tell myself that.

(HARRIET walks over to the chain-link fence and peers out into the darkness.)

BRIAN
Harry, you said you wished we could celebrate Steve's birthday where we always celebrate Steve's birthday, at the Nankin. I went to all this bother—

HARRIET
At the new Nankin, the one down the street—

BRIAN
You said the old Nankin, Harry, I remember.

HARRIET
But our bar isn't here anymore. The restaurant isn't here anymore. (Rummaging through her bag) I'm supposed to have something I don't.

BRIAN
Drink your Wanderer's Punch, Harry. Mine's not quite the same as Jack Woo's, but it's close enough.

(BOTH laugh.)

Stage directions, when to use them and how detailed to make them, is a sticky issue. Just keep in mind what you learned earlier: A play is written to be performed, not read. Trust the intelligence of your fellow collaborators. Too many stage directions in a script and the director, actor, and designer will feel you don't think too highly of their ability to interpret your play, diminishing their enthusiasm about the collaboration. A good general rule about stage directions is to limit them to essential movements, especially entrances and exits ("He walks out the door") and when the meaning of a line or the mood of a moment is vague (e.g., when an "I don't know" really means "yes"). Note also, in stage directions, the name of the character is fully capitalized; this serves to cue the director and the actor playing the character.

The model above provides an example of the standard format for writing play scripts. Use it as a reference for the eight scene-length exercises in the Intermediate Workshop, for writing the full-length play in the Advanced Workshop, and especially when you submit plays to producers, theaters, and contests. Vary the standard format to your tastes and needs, but *always submit a neat ribbon or duplicated copy of the script*. Sad but true: Many times a sloppy or poorly put together script is just tossed aside or read with a prejudiced eye.

In the following two exercises, you'll be turning the scenario you put together in the last exercise into a scene. When working on the scene, you'll be writing two drafts. (Each time you work through the scene completely is a *draft*.) You'll learn as you go along, writing more than anything else is *rewriting*. Many experienced playwrights do draft after draft of a play before they're satisfied. But, for right now, don't frustrate yourself by being too picky, too scrupulous. Doing two drafts will be practice enough.

On the first draft, begin at the beginning of the scene and work through to the end. Don't go back and rewrite any part of the scene until you have finished the first draft. You'll get ideas for changes as you go along, which is good. But, as you work through the first draft, just take notes; follow up on your ideas after you have gone through the entire scene. Too many new playwrights get stuck rewriting and rewriting the first page. Don't worry if the first draft isn't perfect; you can always rewrite later. For now, you need an overall sense of your scene, so keep a forward momentum going.

As you work through your scene the first time, don't stick religiously to your scenario. It is best to lock the scenario in your desk drawer. The dialogue loses its spontaneity when you use the scenario as a "follow-the-dots." Let yourself be free to improvise a little. If you know your raw material inside out and have put together a good scenario, you'll feel all the more confident to take risks.

Let the scene go where it wants. What seems like an improbable tangent might be just where the scene should go. And if the first draft heads in the wrong direction, you can always delete or change what doesn't work—later. Chances are, though, you'll have learned a great deal about your scene by taking that tangent. Feel free to overwrite on the first draft. Most experienced playwrights like to explore every possibility, then return to those tactics and obstacles that best show off the conflict.

Keep in mind that when writing such a short scene, it's not necessary to find a resolution to the conflict. Work instead toward creating a well-balanced, interesting struggle.

And remember, keep pushing through. On the first draft especially, don't get bogged down on something you can't make work. Do what you can, then go on. You can always go back to trouble spots later.

> *Scene Exercise:* Based on your explorations and the scenario you created, write the first draft of a brief scene (approximately five to ten typewritten pages) with a strong, clear-cut conflict between the two characters.

After you have written the entire first draft of the scene, read it over several times, carefully and critically. Read it aloud, at least once. Are the characters consistent? Do they speak for themselves? Are the goals, motivations, and tactics clear? Specific? Interesting? Is the setting well used? Do you think the scene will "hook" the audience right from the opening moments? Is the conflict established right from the opening moments of the scene? Does the scene "hang together"? (Does it move logically from one moment to the next?) Does the scene build, the story becoming more compelling, as the characters and conflict are revealed? Ask all the questions you have learned to ask throughout the Beginning Workshop. Check the first draft against the scenario. Are any additional changes or cuts suggested? Where does the scenario for the scene differ from the scene itself? Why?

For the second draft, you'll want to make any changes you jotted down as you went through the first draft. Focus on trouble spots. Use strategies you have learned throughout the Beginning Workshop to help you find a clear, effective way of solving the problem. (For example, does a character keep using the same *tactic* until it becomes boring? How might you give variety to the tactics that the character uses?) Cut any excess; get down to the heart of the conflict, the core of the story.

Often the hardest thing for new playwrights is to cut what they have written. You have to learn not to think of every word you write as golden. One playwright does all her drafts except her final draft on cheap yellow paper because "cheap yellow paper rips up so easily." Good advice. On the other hand, don't fall into the other trap new playwrights fall into: being *too* hard on yourself, hating everything you write, cutting everything that isn't "perfect."

Second Draft Exercise: Rewrite your first draft.

When you're satisfied with your work, if possible, "cast" the scene—preferably with the two people you used in the last exercise—and have it read aloud. Let a third person read the necessary stage directions. Don't participate in the reading, except as an "audience member." Just listen carefully and objectively. Take notes on trouble spots. (A good sign of a trouble spot is when you find youself wincing.) Does the dramatic situation you invented work? Is the conflict clear? Powerful? Does the story move forward? Are the tactics and obstacles vivid and concrete? And true to the situation? And true to the characters? Is the dialogue natural? Do the characters speak for themselves? Have you used all your building blocks to your best advantage? If you're unhappy with the results, rewrite the scene, making sure every moment of the scene illuminates the basic conflict.

If you enjoy a challenge and want to test your new skills as a playwright, redo the scene, this time placing the scene in the *past* setting from "Creating Settings." Maintain the same relationship between the characters. And the same conflict. Take the scene through the same process you took the first scene. How does the new setting affect the conflict? What new tactics and obstacles do the characters have to come up with?

Your apprenticeship is completed.

You have done some pretty fantastic things. But you still have a lot to learn. The Intermediate Workshop allows you to practice the skills you learned in the Beginning Workshop by doing a series of scene-length exercises that require creativity and ingenuity. Each step of the Intermediate Workshop not only develops basic skills, but also familiarizes you with specific tools and techniques experienced playwrights use to make their work vivid and varied.

CHAPTER TWO

THE INTERMEDIATE WORKSHOP

In the Beginning Workshop, you worked with the basics of playwriting: setting, character, dialogue, conflict, scenario, and writing a scene. The Intermediate Workshop encourages you to develop and refine these fundamental skills through challenging scene-length exercises. Each step of the Intermediate Workshop focuses on a specific tool or technique experienced playwrights use to create vivid, three-dimensional dramatic situations. For example, you'll be writing a scene that is both comic and serious at the same time. (How many times do our lives seem that way!) You'll use setting to reflect the conflict in a scene. You'll create an all-out, no-holds-barred confrontation between two people, then see what happens when you repeat the scene, this time with a third person present. You'll work with scenes involving four, five, even six characters. By the end of the Intermediate Workshop, you'll have a number of critical tools and techniques to help you tackle writing a full-length play in the Advanced Workshop.

You'll find the format of the steps in the Intermediate Workshop similar to that of the steps in the Beginning Workshop, with one important exception: The steps in the Intermediate Workshop are illustrated by models from the plays of experienced playwrights, present and past. You have gone this far. You're serious. It's time to start immersing yourself in plays: reading plays and seeing plays in performance—on a regular basis. Experiencing the work of the masters will both teach and inspire you.

Remember to maintain good working habits. Try to work consistently, preferably every day. Spend no more than two weeks on each step of the workshop, so that you don't lose the continuity of the workshop or get stuck on any one exercise. Don't be discouraged if you feel your work on one or two of the exercises is less than successful. Do the best you can with each scene, put them away in your desk drawer, and come back to them when you have finished the entire workshop. Don't brood about the scenes. Don't let yourself get frustrated. Time, just letting the scenes sit in your subconscious for a while, will usually do the trick. When you finally go back to the scenes, your perspective will be fresh, your attitude better, and your insights sharper. You'll be surprised how quickly you find solutions to obstacles you thought were insurmountable earlier. Experienced playwrights use this technique all the time.

You will begin the Intermediate Workshop by creating a "stock company" of six characters who you will use in the various scenes in the workshop.

Creating a Stock Company

The scenes you'll be working with in the Intermediate Workshop require anywhere from two to six characters. Creating a stock company of six characters from which you "cast" your scenes allows you to review and refine the process for creating characters that you learned in the Beginning Workshop. More important, the stock company encourages you to test your ingenuity and expand your versatility by mixing and matching characters from scene to scene.

In the following exercise you'll be using the processes you learned in "Building Characters," "Putting Your Characters in a Setting," and "Your Characters Talk" in the Beginning Workshop to create six vivid, three-dimensional characters to use in the various intermediate exercises. To strengthen the skills you gained in the Beginning Workshop, three of the characters should be based on total strangers you observe. And the other three characters should be based on people from the past, people with whom you have had some sort of significant emotional relationship—for example, a family member, a close friend, an old flame—but they should be people you haven't seen for a long time. (Doesn't this sound familiar?) Try for variety when choosing the six characters: various ages, several of each sex, different walks of life, and so on.

Once you have picked the six you want to work with, take each character through the process you learned in the Beginning Workshop: Observe or remember the way the character dresses/dressed. Think about the character's daily activities, which reveal so much about his or her personality. Discover how the character talks. Build six complete, three-dimensional characters. When you finish putting the six characters through their paces, you should have the following "dossier" for each character right at your fingertips for easy reference when doing subsequent exercises:

—A short, pithy paragraph about how each character dresses. (Select only the most vivid and revealing details. Be careful not to embellish; be as objective as possible.)

—A brief remembered or invented profile/history of each character.

—A paragraph describing each character doing a revealing action in a setting. (For simplicity's sake, you can use either or both of the settings you worked with in the Beginning Workshop—or, if you like, strengthen your skills by creating several new settings.)

—A 3-minute monologue in which each character describes one of the other five characters, which reveals more about the character *speaking* than the character being described.

Remember, when doing the exercise, to look at each of the six characters carefully and *objectively*. Create six "people" who are interesting and fully rounded, people you look forward to spending the next few months with.

> *Character Exercise:* Create six characters to use in the Intermediate exercises. Three of the characters should be based on people you observe in the present, and three of the characters should be based on people you knew in the past.

Are you satisfied with your stock company? Does it seem balanced? Varied? Lots of interesting people to work with? Good. To test out your stock company, let's try writing a scene with all *six* characters.

Working with Large Groups of Characters

As you learned in the Beginning Workshop, at the heart of every successful scene lies a strong sense of *conflict*. Putting a large group of characters onstage creates a problem of *focus*—how do you include everyone in the conflict?

To solve the problem, experienced playwrights usually make use of a tool called a *central reflector:* one pivotal idea, person, object, place, or event on which all the characters have an opinion. The clash of all the different points of view creates conflict in the scene. *Central reflector?* "Central" because the idea, person, object, or event is pivotal—the focus of the conflict. "Reflector" because what's important is not the idea, person, object, place, or event being discussed, but how the discussion of that idea, person, object, place, or event *reflects* the personalities and relationships of the characters involved in the scene.

Possible central reflectors are limited only by the needs of the scene—usually reflecting the central conflict—and by your imagination.

—If the central reflector is an *idea* or *issue,* for example, it could be an everyday concern such as whether it's okay for people in the same firm to date; it could be a highly emotional issue such as abortion. ("Gloria, you know, one of those Right to Life people tried to get me to sign this petition. I mean, she followed me down the street. . . . Jean, it's her right. . . . It's not, Gloria, it's not her right at all, and just after my sister . . .)

—If the central reflector is an *object,* it could be a rare first edition of James Joyce's *Portrait of the Artist as a Young Man* recently acquired at auction ("Hey, Clarence, I think it's a fake") or simply a missing can of Campbell's Chunky Turkey Soup that Larry wanted for his dinner ("I had my mouth all set for Chunky Turkey; I was virtually drooling as I came up the stairs. You know that's what I have every Thursday for my supper, my Chunky Turkey Soup.")

—If the central reflector is an *event,* it might be a car accident that just happened outside the window. ("Should we go out and help, at least call the police? Or are we going to do what we usually do: not get involved?") It might be a missed birthday party two weeks ago. ("Don't you care about me, at least enough to call me and say you guys aren't coming?") It might be a holiday. Or an event of national or international importance—past, present, or future. ("You're the last person I thought would have sat through all of the Watergate trials.")

—If the central reflector is a *place,* it could be Boston, for example, where the daughter wants to move, but which her family is dead set against. ("Honey, what does Boston offer that Philadelphia doesn't?")

—If the central reflector is a *person,* he or she could be one of the characters onstage, an offstage character, perhaps even an historical figure or celebrity. ("Don't you think Frank Sinatra hit his peak in the early fifties? And now he should just hang it up?" A line like that, stated flatly at the beginning of a scene, would start opinions flying, especially if some people in the group are aging bobby-soxers whose adolescence was one long swoon over "Frankie.")

A good central reflector will not only generate discussion, debate, or conflict, but will also serve as an anchor, giving the scene focus. With opinions about many different topics flying around the stage, an audience can easily become confused, not knowing who to listen to or where the scene is going. A group of people discussing one topic gives the scene unity. Think of the scene as a good volleyball match, where we're just waiting to see how each character handles the "ball" (i.e., the central reflector) when it heads his or her way.

Let's say that for a scene involving four male friends you picked an offstage character, "Andrea," as your central reflector. You have the four men sitting around a kitchen table: Paul, Lennie, Josh, and Everett, all four of whom are involved with Andrea in some way. Andrea recently left Paul. She's just started seeing Paul's friend, Lennie. Josh is Andrea's tough, hot-tempered younger brother, who put the last person that made a crack about Andrea in the hospital. Everett has been infatuated with Andrea since high school, but has always been too shy to admit it.

The four men have had a few too many beers. Still, everyone has been very careful not to talk about Andrea all evening. But Lennie accidentally lets something slip. Paul responds immediately; he talks about Andrea bitterly and abusively. Everett and Lennie have to hold Josh down to stop him from physically attacking Paul. And the fun begins. In the ensuing conflict, Andrea is the central reflector, provoking conflict and revealing who the characters are and their relationship to each other, as well as providing a focal point for the scene.

5th of July, Lanford Wilson's play about the 1960s baby-boom generation growing older and more disillusioned, is almost entirely large group scenes. Appropriately, Wilson uses the Vietnam War—especially the turbulence surrounding America's involvement in the war—as the central reflector in many of the scenes to create conflict, reveal characters and relationships, and anchor the scene. Some of the characters idealize the Vietnam War years, looking back to the time as a kind of Golden Age, a time to be cherished. Some of the characters associate the time with unhappiness—misguided choices and troubled relationships falling apart, a period of their lives best forgotten. The Vietnam years barely touched some of the characters. Some of the characters are too young to remember. And one young character especially doesn't care to hear about it—it's a dead issue.

When the topic of the Vietnam War years comes up—which it frequently does—conflicting memories and differing points of view clash. Through the mirror of the central reflector, through what the characters have to say about an exciting, if difficult, period in American history, the audience learns not so much about the Vietnam War years as who the characters are and their relationship to one another. The central reflector gives the large-group scenes a shape and focus, allowing the audience both to better follow the various major and minor conflicts and to understand the wonderfully complex knot of characters and relationships Wilson has created in *5th of July*.

(When you read or see *5th of July*—which you definitely should—consider too the characters who remain silent when the talk turns to the Vietnam War years. What does their silence reveal about themselves? About their relationship to the other characters in the scene? Note: Silence is a powerful tool. Much as a black-and-white costume attracts the eye in a Technicolor film, a silent character onstage really stands out —a palpable force in a world of conversation.)

Look also at how the master playwrights use the central reflector as a tool in the following plays:

—A cherry orchard, with its haunting memories of the past, its present problems, and its promise of a new Russia to come, is much more than a cherry orchard for the characters in Anton Chekhov's *The Cherry Orchard*. Chekhov's *The Three Sisters* has three alternating, interrelated central reflectors: a *place,* Moscow; an *idea,* time; and an *issue,* work.

—Look at how the characters debate war and money in George Bernard Shaw's *Major Barbara*. Or how the characters wrangle over the issue of class distinction in *Pygmalion* (the play that served as the basis of the musical *My Fair Lady*). Probably more so than any other playwright in this century, Shaw successfully uses *ideas and issues* as central reflectors in his plays. Shaw's genius as a playwright is that he doesn't turn the stage into his soapbox, but instead uses ideas and issues primarily to generate conflict and explore character and relationships.

—In Eugene O'Neill's *The Iceman Cometh,* the character Hickey becomes a central reflector for the large-group scenes whenever he's offstage. A powerful evangelistic personality, Hickey evokes very different responses from the various sordid characters who drink their lives away in the back room of Harry Hope's saloon: Hickey embodies some characters' hope, some characters' salvation, some characters' frustrations, some characters' failures. Hickey polarized characters; Hickey destoys lives; Hickey builds false hopes; Hickey shatters dreams. At the mere mention of Hickey's name, spats, skirmishes, debates, arguments, fights, and brawls erupt.

—Ten thousand dollars in insurance money, the legacy of a grandfather who recently died, provides a compelling central reflector for the struggling inner-city Younger family in Lorraine Hansberry's *A Raisin in the Sun*. In scene after scene, the characters' wrangling over how the insurance money should be spent reveals who the characters are, what the characters want, and what their relationship with each other is.

—In August Wilson's *The Piano Lesson*, an elaborately carved piano that has been passed down through generations of an African American family becomes a catalyst for a brother and sister torn between tradition and survival.

From now on, whenever you're reading or watching a play, look closely at how the playwright uses a central reflector in the large-group scenes.

In the following exercise, you'll be inventing a situation that brings all six characters in your stock company together in conflict in a single scene. As you had to do with the two characters in the first half of the Beginning Workshop, you'll have to use your ingenuity to develop relationships between the six: Are they meeting for the first time? Are they total strangers thrown together by bizarre circumstances? Are they all old friends? All from one family? (Or from two families?) Are three of them family, two friends of the family, and one a stranger? The possibilities are limitless.

You will want to explore the *raw material,* including the environment, the characters, possible activities the characters might be doing in the scene, the relationships of the characters. Develop and refine the conflict through a *scenario*. As you explore and draft the scene, look for an effective, vivid central reflector that best suits the group of characters involved in the scene and the conflict between them. (Would the conflict revolve around an idea? An object? A person? An event? Then what idea? What object? What person? What event? Just what are these people likely to talk about?) As you polish the scene, be constantly aware: Does the central reflector serve as a catalyst for the conflict? Does it focus the conflict throughout the scene? Does it allow us insights into *all* six characters and their relationship to each other? What can you do to make the central reflector more effective? More vivid?

> *Group Character Exercise:* Write a 10- to 15-minute scene using all six characters from your stock company. Use an appropriate central reflector to anchor and focus the scene, reveal character and relationships, and generate conflict.

When you're reasonably satisfied with what you have written, share your work with others. Hold an informal reading with a group of people you feel comfortable with. "Cast" your characters from the group; have everyone else be an audience. Listen carefully as the play is being read. And listen carefully to the comments afterward. (So you don't strain your friendships and family ties by calling people together every week to hear what you have written, finish several exercises in this workshop, then have a coffee-and-doughnuts—wine-and-cheese, champagne-and-strawberries, tea-and-petit-fours, beer-and-pretzels, milk-and-cookies—reading once a month or so of the work you have done up to that point.)

Building Head-to-Head Confrontations

Nothing rivets an audience as much as watching two characters onstage going full tilt at each other in an all-out, no-holds-barred confrontation. Audiences love it! And master playwrights since the Greeks have known how to take full advantage of this tool. Look, for instance, at Euripides' *Medea,* Shakespeare's *The Taming of the Shrew,* or Strindberg's *The Dance of Death*. Edward Albee's vitriolic *Who's Afraid of*

Virginia Woolf? is almost a casebook study of the art of high-voltage confrontations—great fun to read, even more fun to see performed.

In *Who's Afraid of Virginia Woolf?,* the confrontations sometimes are brilliantly comic, laced with acid, or dead serious—weighty, well-aimed punches to the gut and well-timed slams to the side of the head. George, an unsuccessful middle-aged professor, and his brassy, garrulous wife, Martha, are fixtures at a small New England college. Late one night, after a party welcoming the new faculty, they invite Nick, a new, young, go-getter professor, and his wife Honey over for drinks and a little "fun and games." The most popular game that evening is George and Martha's favorite one: verbal abuse. George and Martha are masters of the send-up, the put-down, the taunt, the tease, the invective, vicious jests, verbal barrages, vulgar insinuations, and ridicule. They use each other and their guests as bait. Nick and Honey seem at first easy sport—"pygmy hunting," as George calls it. But the "fun" gets out of hand, the games become much too real, much too painful, the stakes much too high. By morning, the characters are picking their way through the bloody corpses of two disemboweled marriages.

Also look at the clashes, confrontations, and shouting matches in the following recent British and American plays: Tony Kushner's *Angels in America*, David Hare's *Plenty,* Caryl Churchill's *Top Girls,* David Mamet's *Glengarry Glen Ross*, and *Oleanna*, Dennis McIntyre's *Split Second,* Marsha Norman's *'Night, Mother,* Sam Shepard's *Fool for Love,* John Pielmeier's *Agnes of God,* and Wendy Wasserstein's *Isn't It Romantic?*

Great fireworks; great theater. Yet, for some reason, many beginning playwrights shy away from big confrontations. Perhaps it's a fear that if the conflict becomes too big, it will seem embarrassing, phony, "not real." Perhaps it's insecurity about their craft, a fear they can't do justice to outsized emotions.

One way to overcome a fear of writing big confrontations is to get in touch with real-life confrontations. Surely you have experienced, or at least witnessed, turbulent relationships and big confrontations—those moments when your heart races and your mouth goes dry. To prime yourself for the following exercise, think back over some of the major confrontations you remember. As you did way back in "Observing the World as a Playwright" in the Beginning Workshop, using all five senses, jot down as many specific sensory details connected with the confrontations as possible: What was the color of the sweater I really didn't mean to rip off Greg's back when I got mad? What did my best china sound like when Greg decided to be Stanley Kowalski and sweep everything off the table onto the floor? What did the linoleum feel like when we both wound up on the floor? What did Majorie's finger taste like when she stuck it in my face and I tried to bite it off? And Majorie's favorite lemon soufflé I forgot was still in the microwave when we started arguing . . . What did it smell like when it exploded?

As acting students learn early in their training, listing sensory details often triggers your memory of the emotions of a particular moment, especially those "unpleasant" emotions people often suppress. Getting in touch with the emotions involved in confrontations from your own life will help you to understand and shape the confrontations, big and little, that make up your plays.

What follows is a two-part exercise: First, you'll be writing a short confrontation scene between two characters. Then you'll rewrite the scene, seeing what happens when you introduce a third character into the conflict.

You'll be placing any two characters from your stock company in an all-out, no-holds-barred confrontation scene. The tone of the scene can be serious or comic—or, like most of the scenes in *Who's Afraid of Virginia Woolf?*, a little of both. Use the tools and techniques you learned in the Beginning Workshop to explore, draft, and polish the scene. The key word in this kind of scene is *conflict*, so pay particular attention to the tools you first learned in "Putting Together a Basic Scenario": *goal, motivation, obstacles,* and *tactics*. The characters really have to want something. What they want has to be very important. The obstacles have to be particularly overwhelming. And the tactics have to be particularly impressive. For the purposes of this exercise, make the relationship between the two characters one that has always tended to be a little volatile.

When you draft and polish the scene, start with the characters' emotions high and take them higher. Push yourself and your characters to take risks. If you have created two fully rounded characters who have a truly volatile relationship and have put them in a moment where there's a lot at stake for both characters, the scene should virtually write itself. Don't worry about the scene getting out of hand when you're doing the rough draft. Later, when you're polishing the scene, you can rein in the excesses of the scene.

> *Confrontation exercise:* Using any two characters from your stock company, write a 10-minute all-out, no-holds-barred confrontation scene.

After you have written your rough draft, polish the scene by asking yourself the following questions about the characters. If you answer "no" to any of the questions, you'll want to revise accordingly.

—Have their actions remained true to their personalities? Their relationship?

—Are their motivations strong, clear, focused, and consistent? Do they want what they want so much that no one's going to stop them?

—Are the characters' obstacles and tactics *their* obstacles and tactics, not obstacles and tactics imposed on them by you?

—Have the characters made full use of the environment, what they know about each other's strengths and weaknesses, and other elements of the scene as possible obstacles and tactics? (Is there variety to the scene, to the obstacles and tactics used? Or do they keep hammering away at the same things in the same way?)

—Does the conflict build logically?

—Does every moment of the scene illuminate the conflict?

As you polish the scene, make sure you don't get cold feet and begin to undercut the power of the volatile moments between the characters in the rough draft. If anything, if the volatile moments seem "real" and consistent with the characters and their relationship, see if you can beef up those moments—make the moments even bigger. Then use those successful volatile moments as models to give the rest of the scene the same vigor. Go for it—this is theater, after all.

In the next exercise, you'll be asked to redo the scene—same environment, same characters, same conflict, same intensity—but this time adding a third character. The third character can be a stranger, an acquaintance (of one or both of the other characters), or an intimate (of one or both of the other characters). The third character should not be an active participant—someone directly involved with the confrontation. Or at least the character didn't intend to be. Instead the third character might be someone who just walked into the room. Or someone who just happened to be sitting on a nearby park bench when the confrontation began. How does the confrontation change when a third character is present? How does the third character react? Do either or both of the two combatants use the third character as an obstacle? A tactic? ("You agree with me, don't you? Don't you?") Do either or both combatants try to ignore the third character? Does the presence of the third character undermine the power of either or both of the other two characters?

Think back over those confrontations in your life when you were the person who walked into the middle of a fight. Or when a person happened on a real doozy of a fight you and someone were having. Also, you might look through *Who's Afraid of Virginia Woolf?:* Nick and Honey often serve as unwilling spectators/participants in George and Martha's confrontations (and George and Martha often serve as *willing* spectators/participants in Nick and Honey's confrontations!).

> *Three-Character Confrontation Exercise:* Rewrite the two-character confrontation scene above, adding a third character from the stock company as an unwilling—or, if you feel you can handle it, *willing*—spectator/participant.

Primed with a more thorough understanding of the dynamics of such a confrontation, explore, draft, and polish the scene, asking yourself the same questions you asked in the first version of the scene. When you have finished the second scene, compare the two scenes: How are the dynamics of the two scenes different? (Do the two scenes "feel" different?) What new things have you learned about the characters and their relationship? Have you allowed both confrontations to be as "big" as you could?

When you are reasonably satisfied with both scenes, share them with people you trust. Do people react as you hoped they would? Do they think you have gone too far with the confrontation? Not far enough? Why?

Creating Settings that Reflect the Conflict

In the Beginning Workshop, you learned that the setting is crucial to a play, serving as an arena for conflict. Now that you have had some experience working with setting, you're ready to explore another way that playwrights use setting: *to subtly reflect the conflict*. Consider, for example, the relationship of setting and conflict in Henrik Ibsen's *A Doll's House:*

Nora Helmer is the central character in *A Doll's House*. Her conflict is a *choice*: whether she should stay with her husband, who has always treated her like a child and a possession, or go off into the world to discover herself as a woman, as an individual. (Sounds all very modern, doesn't it? But Ibsen wrote the play in 1879.) The setting subtly reflects Nora's conflict. Even before Nora makes her entrance, Ibsen shows us Nora's *choice:* The comfortable home she's built with her husband, well furnished, carpeted, a fire burning in the stove—a "doll's house"—small and perfect and pretty. Or the world outside the window—a snowy winter day, with the harsh, unsympathetic Norwegian night fast approaching.

At the beginning of the play, Nora comes in from outside after a day of shopping, humming, "happy as a little lark" to be back home. As the play progresses, Nora realizes that the cozy world she and her husband have created is not a home at all, but a place where she is treated as something less than human, a mere doll in a doll house. The audience's very last impression of *A Doll's House* is "the door slamming shut" as Nora leaves her "safe, warm" home, maybe forever, choosing to brave the uncertainties awaiting her in the harsh winter night. An heroic act, made even more powerful by Ibsen's use of setting to underscore Nora's choice.

If you have the time, take a close look at *A Doll's House* to see how brilliantly Ibsen uses the setting, as well as costumes and sound effects, to subtly reflect the conflict in every scene.

Also look closely at how the setting reflects the conflict in the following plays:

—In Eugene O'Neill's *Long Day's Journey Into Night,* the sunny morning that opens the play gives way to denser and denser fog to underscore the increasing isolation of the Tyrone family.

—In *Cat on a Hot Tin Roof,* Tennessee Williams uses fireworks and distant thunder to herald the big confrontations.

—In Tina Howe's *Painting Churches,* slowly moving the furniture out of the parlor of a Boston town house through successive scenes captures the bittersweet end of the Church family's life together.

From now on, when you're reading or seeing a play in production, keep a close eye on how experienced playwrights use setting to subtly reflect the conflict.

In the following exercise, you'll be creating a 10- to 15-minute (10- to 15-page) scene, using four characters from your stock company. Use the tools and techniques you learned in the Beginning Workshop to explore, draft, and polish the scene. As you explore the scene, working through the relationship(s) between the four characters, the basic conflict, and so on, begin to think about how you might use the setting, or some element in the setting, to reflect the conflict. Think about what particular kind of setting might *best* reflect the conflict.

For example, four college seniors are graduating, heading off in separate directions, but they're very reluctant to break up the close friendship they have shared for the past several years. Their conflict: to accept change. Perhaps their favorite hangout, a local bar, would reflect this conflict better than the apartment where you first planned to place the scene. Work with the setting; get as much mileage out of it as you can. Perhaps it's past closing and the owner of the bar has already put up the chairs, closed out the cash register, unplugged the jukebox, and turned on the lights, preparing to clean up. Through these subtle details, the setting begins to reflect the conflict, saying, "It's time to break this up, ladies; it's time to be on your way."

As you're exploring the scene, if something brilliant doesn't hit you right away, that's fine. An idea may not hit you until you're drafting or polishing the scene. Give yourself time. Go for a walk. Call a friend and go out dancing. Allow your subconscious to play around with the relationship between the conflict and the setting. If you're like most playwrights, the solution will suddenly seem to come to you from out of the blue. But what's been happening is that all along your subconscious has been working on the problem, weighing this or that possibility, looking for solutions in your daily life. This technique should work for any of the exercises in any of the workshops, and throughout your career as a playwright.

Also, there's a chance you'll change your mind several times about which setting would be best. That's fine, as long as you don't change your mind so many times that you become frustrated. Allow yourself the flexibility to explore and experiment. Just remember (for the following exercise and all the other exercises in the three workshops): You're doing an exercise; you're not trying to write the next Tony Award winner.

Once you have figured out how the setting can be used to reflect the conflict, work through the scene, seeing if you're using the setting to your best advantage: Are you being too subtle? Too obvious? Do you make the relationship of the setting to the conflict *too* central to the scene? (You shouldn't necessarily have the scene be a discussion of how the setting reflects the conflict. More effective, in fact, is to not have anyone in the scene actually comment on the relationship of the setting to the conflict—"The bar closing for the night, it's just like our friendship ending, isn't it?" is the sort of line that often makes an audience grit its collective teeth.) Let the relationship of the setting to the conflict literally be *in the background,* adding texture, tension, and subtle emphasis to the scene.

> *Set Exercise:* Using four characters from your stock company, create a 10- to 15-minute scene that uses the setting as a subtle reflection of the conflict.

When you're reasonably happy with what you have written, share the scene with people whose opinions you value. Do they *see* how the setting reflects the conflict? Ask them if they think they could better visualize how the setting reflects the conflict if they actually saw the scene staged. (Remember, it's difficult for most people to read a play, and it's especially difficult to visualize what a scene will *look like* onstage. In exercises like this, you may have to depend on your own judgment of what works and what doesn't. And, at this point in the process of your becoming a playwright, that's not a bad thing.)

Balancing the Comic and the Serious in a Scene

When you have listened to two people bickering on the bus, have you had to struggle to keep from laughing because of the sheer silliness of what they have been arguing about for the past half hour? "The color of her hat was beige. . . . No, Patsy, you're wrong; the hat was wheat. . . . Everyone knows you're blind as a bat, Ellie; it was beige, beige as my skirt. . . . Your skirt isn't beige; it isn't wheat either, Patsy; it's more of a cream. . . ."

Or, have you ever been so mad at your sister that you picked up the veal chop you were defrosting for dinner and were about to hurl it across the kitchen at her, when suddenly you realized just what it was you were about to hurl? And you started to laugh. And your sister started to laugh, even though there were tears of anger and frustration in both your eyes. Life is full of moments when you don't know whether to laugh or cry, which are both funny and painful. And experienced playwrights realize that these kinds of moments make great theater. Scenes that are funny and painful at the same time are invariably audience pleasers. The push and pull of what's comic and what's serious in the scene creates a *dynamic* that adds variety and emotional texture to the scene. Good plays, even the airiest comedies and the darkest tragedies, blend serious and comic elements to give the overall play balance and perspective.

Case in point: *Long Day's Journey Into Night,* Eugene

O'Neill's bleak portrait of the Tyrone family; no sane person would call it a comedy, yet there are many comic moments—even when the play is at its darkest. For instance, O'Neill includes a scene where Mary Tyrone shares confidences and her husband's whiskey with the young Irish maid, Cathleen; the scene confirms the horror of Mary's slide back into her morphine addiction, but Cathleen's gossipy drunkenness is pure vaudeville. The interlude makes you laugh, despite your-self.

The lighter moments in a serious play allow the audience a necessary respite from the inexorable machine of tragedy, time to stand back and comprehend the full scope of the play. Much the same are those moments in a comedy when the audience is allowed to glimpse the potential darkness under all the fun. Training yourself to be comfortable with combining the comic and the serious in a scene will be invaluable when you start working on full-length plays, when you start taking a story over the long haul and need a technique to help create variety and contrast.

Beth Henley's Pulitzer Prize–winning comedy, *Crimes of the Heart,* skims along nicely between outrageous comedy and devastating pathos throughout its three acts. Toward the end of *Crimes of the Heart* comes a wonderful comic/serious scene. Their world tumbling down around them, two sisters, Babe and Lenny, are so exhausted, so broken by a series of tragedies, that when they try to tell their other sister, Meg, of yet *another* tragedy—their granddaddy's stroke—they laugh instead of cry. Then, of course, they feel guilty and try to act morose, but wind up laughing again. Every night the Broadway audience went right along with the sisters, laughing, the laughter freezing on the face, guilt creeping in, then helplessly laughing again, back and forth—a real roller coaster ride. When you read or see a performance of *Crimes of the Heart,* think about how maudlin and uninteresting the scene would have been handled heavy-handedly, or even reverentially.

A few other examples of the many ways you can use the comic and the serious in a scene can be found in the following plays: Noel Coward's sophisticated *Private Lives*—or its more modern counterpart, Tom Stoppard's *The Real Thing;* Anton Chekhov's at times almost farcical *The Cherry Orchard*; Wendy Wasserstein's family portrait, *The Sisters Rosensweig*; John Guare's acid-etched *Six Degrees of Separation*; Eugene O'Neill's gently nostalgic, *Ah, Wilderness!*—especially the scene where Uncle Sid comes drunk to the dinner table. Also, Edward Albee's free-for-all, *Who's Afraid of Virginia Woolf?*, where almost every moment in the play is invariably very funny and inevitably very sad.

From now on, when you're reading a play or seeing a play performed, think about how, when, and why the playwright blends comic and serious elements in the play.

When writing a scene that is both comic and serious, a playwright needs to keep two things in mind:

—What is the *situation* that makes the scene *serious?* Is the scene a confrontation? A last good-bye? A petty argument? A naive political discussion? An act of revenge?

—*How* is the scene *comic?* Does the scene depend on *verbal humor:* Are either or both of the characters using wit and cleverness to express (or not express) anger? Hostility? Hurt? Frustration? Or perhaps it's just the opposite: The scene is comic because either or both characters are so angry, hurt, frustrated, serious, obsessed, or hostile that, try as they may, they *cannot* find the words to say what they want to say.

Does the scene depend on *physical humor:* Are the characters fumbling, stumbling, crashing about the stage in their efforts to express (or not express) anger? Hurt? Frustration? Suppose, for example, Rachel is moving out on Dennis. Dennis doesn't want Rachel to leave and Rachel really doesn't want to leave. But there's just one last box of her belongings to tape up and she'll be on her way. One problem: Try as they may, neither one is able to get any tape off the roll of tape. Without realizing what they're doing, both Dennis and Rachel begin to dump their hurt and frustration about leaving each other on the poor roll of tape.

They do everything they can to get that damn tape off the roll. The harder they try, the funnier the scene becomes.

Comic/Serious Exercise: Using two characters from your stock company (ther than the three you used in "Building Head-to-Head Confrontations"), create a 10- to 15-minute scene that is outwardly comic, although the situation is serious for one or both of the characters.

Polish the scene, using the tools and techniques you have learned up to this point—including those tools and techniques you studied in the Intermediate Workshop. As you polish, look closely at the relationship of the serious and the comic in the scene: Does having the scene be both comic and serious *add to* the conflict? Does the push and pull of the comic and the serious enrich the conflict, giving the scene more vitality? Does it give the conflict variety? (Making the audience laugh one moment, hurt the next is a wonderful way of keeping their attention, constantly interested in what's happening onstage.) Does the comedy arise out of the situation? Out of the characters and their relationship? Be sure the comedy does not seem forced and unnatural—or "jokey." Put the right characters in the right situation and they will be funny without even trying.

When you feel good about the scene, try it out on friends. Do they laugh? Do they sometimes feel a little uncomfortable laughing because of the situation? (If so, that's usually a good sign that the scene is having the effect you want.) Do they find the humor comes naturally out of the situation? The characters? The relationship of the characters? Or does the humor seem forced? Why? Is your "audience" aware of the seriousness of the situation beneath the comedy? If not, why not?

Harnessing the Power of the Unresolved Conflict

Perhaps the most powerful conflict onstage is the unresolved conflict. An unresolved conflict is one that began sometime in the past. Circumstances prevented the conflict from being resolved. And it lay unresolved for years. For example, Lonnie betrayed his best friend Jerry, then left town before Jerry had a chance to confront him. Jerry's bewilderment grew into bitterness. Lonnie thought the guilt he felt would abate, but it just grew stronger as the years went by. The two men meet again, years later, at the funeral of a mutual friend. Old hostilities resurface. Suppressed emotions can no longer be contained. The conflict that should have been resolved years ago explodes across the stage. Heavy-duty stuff; and audiences just eat it up.

Two things happen that make an unresolved conflict such powerhouse drama, and both involve the element of *time:*

—*Time* allows bad feelings to fester. Usually, as much as we may try to repress our feelings, grievances that are not allowed to be aired consume us. Unanswered questions and lingering doubts haunt us. Emotions that have never been allowed to be expressed get bottled up inside us, aching to be released. So that when the chance finally comes to express our feelings, *stand back!*

—*Time* distorts the original incident. The unresolved conflict is colored by our strongly subjective "bad memories" of the original incident. The more time goes by, the more distorted our perception becomes, the more we tend to remember what we *want* to remember. The clash of several people's memories of the original incident makes for great emotional fireworks.

Just how powerful a tool unresolved conflict is can be seen in Arthur Miller's *Death of a Salesman*. Willy Loman and his son Biff have become estranged over an incident in a Boston hotel room many years earlier. The incident, Biff finding his father with another woman, shattered Willy and Biff's close relationship, and led to Biff's throwing away a bright future in sports, his life becoming essentially a waste. When Willy and Biff confront each other, the unresolved conflict ultimately affects not only the two men but all the other characters in the universe of the play. If you haven't done so already, read or, better, see *Death of a Salesman;* it's a powerful portrait of a troubled relationship.

Other fine examples of the power of unresolved conflict can be found in the following plays: Tony Kushner's *Angels in America*, August Wilson's *Joe Turner's Come and Gone*, Harold Pinter's *Old Times* (or, for that matter, *The Homecoming* or *Betrayal*—Pinter loves to play games with unresolved conflict), Tennessee Williams' *Cat on a Hot Tin Roof* (especially the powerful confrontation between Maggie and Brick in the first half of the first act), and Athol Fugard's *A Lesson From Aloes*.

From now on, when you're reading or seeing a play, pay close attention to see if and how the playwright uses unresolved conflict.

To prepare yourself emotionally for creating a situation involving unresolved conflict, think back over your life to incidents that involved unresolved conflict. Practice what you reviewed earlier in the Intermediate Workshop: Using all five senses, jot down as many specific sensory details connected with the incidents as possible. Listing sensory details often triggers your memory of the emotions connected with a particular incident, especially those unpleasant emotions people usually suppress. Getting in touch with the emotions involved in unresolved conflicts from your own life will help you to understand and shape the unresolved conflict you create in this exercise.

When writing a scene that revolves around an unresolved conflict, you need to consider the following:

—How much time has elapsed since the original conflict and the present?

—What brought the characters back together? Did they meet again by accident? Through circumstances beyond their control? Was their getting back together arranged by one or more of the characters? (It would be a totally different scene depending on which character(s) brought everyone back together again. *Motivation* becomes a critical factor in scenes involving unresolved conflict.)

—How does the past affect the present characters? The present relationship(s)? The present conflict? For example, what is the emotional state of each character when the scene begins? What does each character *want?*

—What are the dynamics of the scene? Does the scene start out polite and stay polite? Or does it end up with fists flying and hair-pulling? Do the characters dislike each other from the moment they meet?

—How do the characters try to use the past to their advantage? (As *tactics?* As *obstacles?*) Do the characters distort the past? On purpose? Because of the emotions they've kept suppressed?

—Is the conflict resolved? (It doesn't have to be. It's often more realistic if it isn't fully resolved, especially in such a short scene.)

Always *use* the past to further the *conflict*. Whenever the original incident is brought up, it should be used by the characters as either a *tactic* or an *obstacle*—to achieve or to prevent someone from achieving his or her *goal* in the present. (If you're still a little unsure of such terms as *tactic, obstacle, motivation,* and *goal,* review for a few minutes "Putting Together a Basic Scenario" in the Beginning Workshop.)

Also, don't worry whether the audience gets a complete picture of what happened in the past. Remember: Memory, especially of highly emotional incidents, is both subjective and selective, and usually becomes even more so as time goes by. *How* the characters remember the past incident is the key to an unresolved conflict. Keeping the audience a little in the dark, constantly making them curious as to "what really happened," is a marvelous technique for holding their attention. Just think back over every Perry Mason episode that held you in suspense and you'll understand the power of the unresolved conflict: "Annette, I'm sure it was all his fault. . . . No, Peter, I'm sure she's not telling the truth. She may think she's telling the truth, but she's not. Look at him; he's obviously much more trustworthy. . . ."

> *Unresolved Conflict Exercise:* Take two to four characters from your stock company. (Try to use characters you haven't used much yet.) Create a 15- to 20-minute scene in which an old conflict is unearthed and rehashed in the present.

When you're ready, try out the scene on family and friends. Do they find that the scene holds their attention? That the circumstances which brought the characters together are believable? That the conflict has a particular intensity? What do they learn about the characters? Their relationships? Their history? Why?

Understanding the Relationship of Ritual and Drama

Understanding the relationship between ritual and drama is the key to successful playwriting. When you hear the word *ritual,* you probably think of *religious* ritual—the ceremonies practiced week after week, year after year, in churches. And, to a degree, you're right. The earliest drama emerged out of religious rituals; Greek drama and medieval European drama show a close tie to the religions of the time. But modern drama, for the most part, has moved away from religious ritual to smaller, everyday rituals: *social* rituals, *family* rituals, and *personal* rituals.

The dictionary defines ritual as "any detailed method of procedure faithfully or regularly followed." Examples of ritual might be as diverse as an induction into a secret society, dinner every Sunday with Nana Rosie, stopping off at Shakey's on your way home from work on Friday, even how you remove your makeup before going to bed. Whether they are as simple as who uses the bathroom first every morning or as involved as an old-fashioned wedding—with its weeks, often months, of preparations—rituals give our lives a certain pattern and order and meaning.

Sometimes consciously, sometimes unconsciously, we use rituals as an outline for performing the big and little activities that make up our lives. We like rituals because they are familiar, comfortable; we know pretty much what to expect each time we perform an activity. Rituals allow us to say, "This is who I am. This is where I should be. And this is what I should be doing at this particular time." Consider the following examples of social, family, and personal rituals:

—*Social rituals:* For the past three years, five fairly close friends have met at Ernie's Bar on Thursdays after work for "attitude adjustment hour." Or Margaret and Fred Dumont have played pinochle with Leonora and Sherman Helmsley every other Wednesday since 1958, and except for vacations, births, and that hurricane in August of 1962, rarely, if ever, miss a match.

—*Family rituals:* Every Christmas Eve since Majorie was a baby, her family, the Zaiks, has gone to 7:30 Mass at the Episcopal church, then to Aunt Letitia's for a buffet. Or, at the Gunnings', Ken always makes the pancakes on Sunday mornings—he's too fussy to let anyone else cook—while Lesley goes out to get the paper. (Of course, Lesley would really like to cook Sunday breakfast herself some of the time—especially since she's not fond of pancakes, especially Ken's.)

—*Personal rituals:* Getting dressed in the morning, Mason always puts on one sock then his shoe, then the other sock and the other shoe. Sam, his roommate at Virginia Wesleyan, puts on both socks, then both shoes. Ever since the school year began, Mason has asked himself why Sam gets dressed that way. Sam doesn't even notice that Mason puts his shoes and socks on differently. (It drives Sam crazy, however, that Mason swallows his toothpaste instead of spitting it out, "like normal people do.") Or, for years now, every time Ronnette Grady comes in the door from work, she turns on the television. She rarely watches television, but she likes the set on all the time, with the volume low, "for company."

Read any script, watch any production, and you'll see that plays always focus on *disrupted rituals*. Almost all people need—*require*—their lives to be relatively calm, to go along smoothly. People naturally tend to be uncomfortable with change because change is threatening. Most people then, consciously or unconsciously, work very hard to maintain the status quo, to "keep things the way they are." Rituals reinforce the status quo by giving people a repeated pattern to their lives. ("Every one of my daughters has been married in the Catholic church, and my Joan is going to be too, or it'll be over my dead body.") When someone or something disrupts that ritual, people are shaken up, lives are thrown off balance, ideas are brought into question. ("Joan, let's elope; I know a swell justice of the peace in Maryland who . . . But Howard, my *father* . . .") Whether major or minor, the disruption *creates conflict;* the characters are forced to deal with the disruption in order to return to a state of equilibrium, either by trying to return to the way things were or by creating new rituals to replace the disrupted rituals. ("Joan, why can't we let the baby celebrate both Christmas and Chanukah?") Think about what might happen if someone or something disrupted the rituals described above. For example:

—What might happen if a new person who nobody really liked joined the group on Thursday for "attitude adjustment hour"? Or an inept burglar climbed in through the window right in the middle of a pinochle match at the Helmsleys'?

—What might happen to the Zaiks' Christmas Eve if Aunt Letitia moved to Nevada? Or Ken woke up Sunday morning to find Lesley making omelettes?

—What might happen if Ronnette came home and found her television wouldn't work? If a repairman couldn't come for at least four days? And no matter what she tried to do to occupy herself, she felt a little lonely? Maybe she'd start doing what she's never done before: going for a walk after dinner. Maybe she would pass Mr. Shaw, her neighbor down the block. Maybe she'd ask him a little tartly why he never weeds his lawn. Maybe Mr. Shaw would ask her over for dinner tomorrow evening. Maybe Ronnette's life would change completely.

Anything is possible, even when the smallest personal ritual is disrupted; that's why the disrupted ritual is such a powerful playwriting tool.

Much of the power of Tennessee Williams' *A Streetcar Named Desire* comes from Williams' deft handling of disrupted rituals—literally every kind of ritual from the cosmic to the seemingly insignificant is disrupted over the course of the play, each disruption adding more and more heat to the central conflict between Blanche DuBois and Stanley Kowalski. The conflict? Simply stated, Stanley Kowalski has a very strong sense of territory, of what and who belongs to him—this includes his apartment, his wife Stella, and his rough-and-tumble lifestyle in the French Quarter of New Orleans.

Into Stanley's world comes Stella's sister, Blanche, who, although she seems very much the fragile Southern spinster, is in many ways as strong and determined a fighter as Stanley. Half consciously, half unconsciously, Blanche becomes an interloper, encroaching on Stanley's domain by *disrupting the rituals,* big and little, that define his world: Blanche intrudes on Stanley's sacred all-night poker games. Blanche's presence in the tiny apartment brings to a virtual halt the lovemaking rituals ("making the colored lights go round") that define Stanley and Stella's relationship. Blanche undermines Stanley's role as a husband and his future role as a father. Blanche even disrupts Stanley's smallest day-to-day rituals—like his bathroom ritual; she dominates the space day and night with *her* ritual: soaking in a hot tub for her nerves (*perfect,* because the play's central conflict revolves around territoriality!).

Stanley, of course, wants things back the way they were before Blanche arrived; he wants to rid himself of this trespasser, this interloper on his territory. As the play's conflict turns in Stanley's favor, Stanley does more than disrupt Blanche's rituals, he brutally violates them. For instance, toward the end of the play, at Blanche's birthday "celebration," Stanley stridently upsets protocol by rudely eating dinner with his fingers, not entering into the expected conviviality of the occasion, and, when Stella complains that he is being a "pig," Stanley violently throws dishes to the floor. The topper, though, is Stanley's birthday present to Blanche. Stanley turns Blanche's *ritual expectations* upside down. Blanche tremulously opens the present: a bus ticket back to Laurel—back to where she has run away from!

When you have a chance, also look at how the following master playwrights use disrupted ritual in their plays.

—Caryl Churchill's *Top Girls:* The celebration of a woman executive's recent promotion in a London employment agency is disrupted by an unexpected arrival: the woman's daughter, whom she abandoned as an infant in order to pursue her career.

—Henrik Ibsen's *The Wild Duck:* The relative domestic harmony of the Ekdal household is shattered by a new boarder, an old childhood friend of the husband's, who believes the Ekdal's marriage is founded on a lie that must be brought to light.

—Simon Gray's *Otherwise Engaged:* Simon Hench just

wants to spend a quiet weekend afternoon listening to his new recording of Wagner's *Parsifal*. A string of intrusions from people out of his past and present does more than just ruin Hench's afternoon—it forces him to confront his own lack of humanity.

—Eugene O'Neill's *The Iceman Cometh:* Each year, the much-loved Hickey makes Harry Hope's birthday party a riotous drunkfest. This year, however, Hickey has something entirely different in mind for Hope's birthday.

From now on, when you're reading a play or seeing a play in production, pay particularly close attention to how experienced playwrights use disrupted rituals to create conflict. Look for big rituals and small rituals; you'll be surprised how many you find.

To prepare yourself for using ritual in a scene, think back over the disrupted rituals, major or minor, you have experienced or witnessed. What was the ritual? Was it a social ritual? A family ritual? A personal ritual? (Perhaps it was even a religious ritual.) What disrupted the ritual? How did the people react? What conflict(s) did the disruption create? Was the conflict resolved? How was it resolved? How did the disruption change the people involved? The relationships? As you did earlier, focus on the five senses when thinking back to disrupted rituals you have experienced or witnessed. Conjuring up sense memories is a perfect tool for unlocking emotional memories while, at the same time, allowing you to remain as objective as possible about the incident being remembered.

Now, begin to think about a scene you could write in which a ritual would be disrupted. Think of an appropriate ritual. It should be a significant ritual for one, some, or all of the characters in the scene. If you have trouble thinking of an appropriate ritual, do what experienced playwrights do: Borrow from your life. A disrupted ritual based on a real situation can be so much more vivid and three-dimensional than one you have invented. And, at this point, it should be easy for you to do what most experienced playwrights do: Adapt a real-life disrupted ritual so it works with the fictional characters you have chosen from your stock company. One nice side benefit of using an actual situation: When you're stuck, there's always the original ritual, with its specific sense and emotional memories, to draw from and inspire you.

> *Ritual Exercise:* Using at least four characters from your stock company, create a 15-minute scene that centers on a disrupted ritual.

As you prepare to polish your scene, ask yourself the following questions:

—What is the ritual? Is it a social ritual? A family ritual? A personal ritual? What is the *scenario* of the ritual? (What usually happens, step-by-step, when the ritual is performed? How and when does it begin? How and when does it end? And so on. Ask yourself the same questions you would ask about a play scenario.)

—Are there ever any significant variations on the basic scenario of the ritual? (When the Dumonts play pinochle with the Helmsleys every other Wednesday, do the two couples sometimes go out to dinner before? Do the Dumonts sometimes drive over? Sometimes take the bus? And so on.)

—How does each character respond to the ritual? What may be very important to one character may mean very little to another. For example, that group of five who meet every Thursday afternoon for attitude adjustment hour. For one of the group, Grady, it's his only chance to see Lea Ann—with whom he's been secretly in love for the past four years—outside the office. On the other hand, Cindy goes mostly to hear some good gossip and to munch on those great chicken wings Ernie serves. If the ritual is disrupted, the stakes are obviously much higher for Grady than they are for Cindy.

—What disrupts the ritual? A person? An event? The weather? An idea? A thing? (Like Ronnette's television going on the blink.) If it's someone, is the someone an outsider? Or someone involved in the ritual? (Ira has always been second banana to Vinnie in their group. Tonight Ira's decided there's going to be a few changes made. . . .)

—When and how is the ritual disrupted? What are the specific circumstances? For example, if a ritual is disrupted before it even begins, the scene might be very different than if the ritual is disrupted as it is happening. (The pinochle game at the Helmsleys' being canceled because the Helmsleys' house was burgled during the afternoon is very different from having a burglar enter when the Dumonts and the Helmsleys are in the middle of a match.)

—How does the disruption affect the ritual? The characters? The relationships? Immediately? As the scene progresses?

—What *conflict* does the disruption generate? Do one, some, or all of the characters try to get rid of the disruption? (Grady thinks the new guy in the group is trying to make a play for Lea Ann, so he's trying very hard to convince the guy to leave.) Do one, some, or all of the characters ignore the disruption? Barely notice the disruption? Go along with the disruption? (Cindy's glad to see a new person join the group on Thursdays; she was getting a little bored seeing the same old faces week after week. Besides, the new guy's kind of cute.) Is the conflict strictly between those in the ritual and the disruption? Or does conflict also occur between various characters involved in the ritual? (Cindy chides Grady, saying he's being rude to the new guy because he's jealous. Grady blows up. Lea Ann begins to realize . . .)

—Are any or all the conflicts resolved? Does the ritual change significantly? Permanently? Are characters and relationships affected? Permanently? Does the old ritual stay pretty much intact? Or does it fall apart? Does a new ritual evolve (or start to evolve) to replace the old one? If a new ritual evolves, does it (or will it) include all the characters in the original ritual? Less? More?

When you are reasonably satisfied with your work, share it with others. Listen carefully and objectively to their reactions, opinions, and suggestions. By this time, you should be making more and more contacts in the theater world (at the community theater, college, or professional level), finding actors, directors, and designers whose input will be particularly helpful. Experienced playwrights often find it best to show their work-in-progress to both theater artists and people who don't have that much theater savvy. Theater artists tend to focus in on certain, often more technical aspects of a script; people outside theater tend to see other, often more "emotional" aspects of the script, treating the script as a slice of real life. Together, they give you a more complete picture of your work.

Face it: Many of the exercises in the Intermediate Workshop have been downright *hard!* If you handled those all right, you're more than ready to attack a full-length play. But think how far you have come. Think back over the last two workshops, at all the tools and techniques you've learned and practiced. The Advanced Workshop will give all the freedom you need to put what you have learned to work. Feel secure that you now have a solid base to begin making more and more of your own creative decisions. So, with your sleeves rolled up, pencil in hand . . . Shall we?

CHAPTER THREE

THE ADVANCED WORKSHOP

The Advanced Workshop guides you through the process of writing a full-length script. (A full-length play is considered a full evening's entertainment, about 1½ to 2 hours playing time—typed, scripts usually run about 90 to 120 pages.) You'll begin the process by spending some time thinking about what's important to you, what you feel a need to speak out about in a full-length play. Then you'll look back over your life for characters, relationships, and stories that might serve as a basis for your play. You'll create several scenarios, so you can fully work out the plot and fill in the details before actually writing any dialogue. You'll experiment with writing exploratory first and last scenes in order to get a sense of where your play is going and where it will end up. Then you'll write the play. You'll rewrite the play. And you'll polish the play.

The Advanced Workshop will feel a bit different from the Beginning and Intermediate Workshops. The Advanced Workshop provides you with greater freedom to develop and refine the tools and techniques you have learned up to now. You'll find less detailed explanations of what to do and how to do it. But don't panic. Because the Advanced Workshop builds upon the two previous workshops, you can always refer back to earlier steps if you feel you're having problems with, say, fleshing out a character, or developing a conflict. Feel confident; you're going into this with a *lot* of preparation. No doubt, after two workshops' worth of "what to do and how to do it," you'll find the freedom the Advanced Workshop allows you exhilarating.

After all this discussion of the freedom you'll have in the workshop, let's talk about two major *restrictions* you'll be asked to observe. First, true to the other two workshops, you'll be asked, whenever possible, to draw the material of the play from your life—from people you have known, events you have witnessed, places you have lived in or traveled through. You have had practice using your observations and insights as raw material for scenes in the last two workshops; you know how much more rich, vivid, and three-dimensional your scenes become when you borrow from life. Of course, having this restriction might make you want to rethink your idea about the play with Princess Zara set on Neptune in the twenty-third century. (But, then again, if Princess Zara reminds you of your middle sister . . .) A good straightforward play, built on firsthand observations and deeply felt emotions and insights, is a fine way to start off a "career" as a playwright. Just ask O'Neill or Ibsen or Shaw or Marsha Norman. . . .

The second restriction concerns the form of the play. Modern full-length plays are usually written either one of two ways: in one or two (sometimes three) continuous acts ("continuous" meaning having all the action in an act take place in the same setting and the time passing onstage mirroring the passing of real time). Or in a number (anywhere from four or five to fifty or more) of scenes, often grouped together into two (rarely three) acts. Over the past two decades, writing in scenes has gained ascendancy over writing in continuous acts. The reasons for this shift to plays in scenes are many, including an increased freedom—or "looseness"—in theatrical form as a whole, as well as the influence of cinema, with its technical innovations such as cross-cutting and split-screen, which modern playwrights have ingeniously modified for the stage. In the middle of the nineteenth century, plays were written in five acts. Over time, the five-act structure gave way to four acts; three acts were popular during the 1920s and 1930s; and, by the late 1940s, a two-act structure prevailed. Over the last decade, writing plays in two continuous acts has begun to give way to extended one-act plays and plays written in short, discrete scenes (lights up, scene . . . lights down . . . lights up, new scene).

Both the more old-fashioned continuous act and the more modern scene-by-scene methods of telling the story of a play are fine. Both have their strengths and weaknesses. In this workshop, you'll be asked to be very modern and write your play in scenes (you can then, if you wish, group into acts where a natural break in the action occurs) for a number of very practical reasons:

—Writing a play in one or two continuous acts is more difficult than writing a play in scenes. Because the action is continuous, you constantly have to worry about the mechanics of getting characters on and off stage without the reality of the play being strained.

—Rewriting is particularly difficult; if you make a change, often the whole act has to be reworked. If you're writing the play in scenes, you create a progression of conflicts. When a particular conflict is over, you end the scene. Blackout. Lights up. Another scene. If one scene—one conflict—isn't working, take out the scene and rework it or replace it. (Think of the process as modular playwriting!)

—Writing the play in scenes also allows you more freedom to incorporate the tools and techniques you have learned up to this point. For instance, you might place each scene in a different setting, allowing you to practice creating settings. And each setting might reflect the conflict in a different way. Perhaps one scene might employ a certain disrupted ritual, and the next scene a completely different disrupted ritual. Perhaps one scene has a large group of characters and an interesting central reflector. And the next scene might then be a head-on confrontation between two of the characters. And the scene following that might have a serious/comic flavor. The possibilities to experiment and play around with what you have learned up to now are limitless.

Writing a play in scenes (and then grouping the scenes into acts, if you wish) instead of writing in one or two continuous acts is the best way to approach your first play: Quite simply, a play in scenes is simpler to write, simpler to rewrite, and simpler to polish. And, by writing a play in scenes grouped into acts, you're actually preparing yourself for writing a play in continuous acts. Look at plays written in acts, such as Ibsen's *A Doll's House,* Chekhov's *The Cherry Orchard,* or Lanford Wilson's *5th of July,* and you'll see the acts are really a progression of scenes skillfully interwoven to look like one long, continuous action. So, when you're more comfortable with writing full-length plays, you can, if you wish, readily make the transition to writing in acts instead of scenes. (More about this at the end of the workshop.)

(Note: If you feel you absolutely must write your first play in two or three continuous acts, you're free to do so. Just think of the various encounters, confrontations, and incidents as linked scenes instead of a sequence of separate scenes. All the steps in the Advanced Workshop will apply; just modify the process for your particular needs.)

In order to have a better understanding of what a full-length play in five or more scenes looks like before you begin the Advanced Workshop, read or see in performance at least several of the following plays. Some of the plays are broken down into scenes, some into scenes *and* acts:

Tony Kushner's *Angels in America*
Tennessee Williams' *The Glass Menagerie* and *A Streetcar Named Desire*

Craig Lucas' *Prelude to a Kiss*
Jay Presson Allen's *The Prime of Miss Jean Brodie*
William Gibson's *Two for the Seesaw*
Dennis McIntyre's *Split Second*
David Hare's *Plenty*
David Mamet's *Sexual Perversity in Chicago*
Harold Pinter's *Betrayal* (A riveting experiment: The scenes go backward in time over several years. The play opens with the aftermath of a love triangle and goes back through the years to the moment the triangle started.)
Terrence McNally's *Love! Valour! Compassion!*
Beth Henley's *The Miss Firecracker Contest*
Tom Stoppard's *The Real Thing* (and, if you're adventurous, his difficult but rewarding *Arcadia*)
Amlin Gray's *How I Got That Story*
John Guare's *Six Degrees of Separation*
Tina Howe's *The Art of Dining*
Bill C. Davis' *Mass Appeal*
Wendy Wasserstein's *The Heidi Chronicles*
Brian Friel's *Dancing at Lughnasa*
Lanford Wilson's *The Rimers of Eldritch* (A particularly ambitious and poetic use of the scene-by-scene format. The scenes go back and forth in time over a spring, summer, and fall. The play involves an entire town. Several secondary stories revolve around a central story.)

Defining Your Vision

Plays come from the playwright's *experience,* nowhere else. The vast experience of your life will shape each play you write and give the play a depth, resonance, and vitality that only you, having lived the life you have, can bring to the play. Everything that touches your life becomes part of your imagination, part of your playwriting: the places you have visited, the events you have witnessed, the people you have come in contact with, the ideas and prejudices you have learned over the years. Your *experience* shapes the way you view life. And everyone's experience, no matter how similar it seems on the outside, is very, very different.

Suppose, for example, you're a playwright who's firmly rooted in "middle-class America." Certainly your experiences are different from someone who grew up in poverty-stricken rural Appalachia or someone who spent her childhood summering in a forty-four-room "cottage" in Newport, Rhode Island. But also remember, if you grew up in the middle-class Bensonhurst section of New York City, you will develop a different way of viewing life than if you were raised in a middle-class neighborhood in Akron, Ohio. Even if in both cases your father was a laid-off machinist, your mother was a part-time legal secretary, you had two brothers and a sister, a 1965 Chevy Caprice, and all other aspects of your life matched exactly. Even if you grew up across the street from yourself, you'd be a much different person than you are now, with very different experiences and a different vision of life.

Even if you and your identical twin both became playwrights—same household, exact same upbringing—you both would write very different plays. Because each of you is different—each of you has his or her own personality, each of you has had a distinct set of experiences, each of you has developed your own special way of seeing the world. (Your identical twin never had that wonderful talk you had with Uncle Latham one afternoon when you were ten about how a star emerged out of the darkness and how a star died, a talk that changed how you looked at life . . . a lot. Your identical twin never glimpsed that old woman hawking two-day-old newspapers outside Dayton's, a glimpse that changed how you looked at life . . . a little.)

But it's interesting: People don't like to think of themselves as unique and special. The majority of us try very hard not to be different: we move with the pack ("But everyone's buying . . ."); we put ready-made, easily identifiable labels on ourselves ("I'm just your typical jock . . ."); we try to conform to what we think "our type of person" should be ("Women like me don't . . ."). You know what's wonderful though: Try as we may not to be different, we're different—with quirks, idiosyncracies, and prejudices all very much our own. You learned in the Beginning Workshop when creating characters to look at other people as individuals, to notice the subtle differences that make each person *unique and special*. It's time to look at yourself as a *unique and special* writer who has a *unique and special* history and has developed a *unique and special* way of seeing the world.

At the risk of having this sound like cheap psychobabble, the biggest obstacle most beginning playwrights have to face when they sit down to write is accepting the fact that they have a unique and special way of looking at the world, and that they have something important to share with an audience. ("What? My play? Let's not read it; it's not nearly as interesting as Mandy's . . . I mean, her life has been so fascinating, filled with all this *drama;* she has so much to say; and she sees things in people and relationships I could never see . . .")

Your "unique and special way of seeing the world" is called your *vision*. Although you'll be asked later to try to define your vision in one brief statement, your vision is actually very complex, the sum total of every person, place, and thing, tangible and intangible, that has touched your life. No matter what you write about, your vision will be present. Given an experience or event to write a play about, you'll filter the raw material through your vision, bringing to the raw material your ideas, your point of view, the distillation of all your experiences. Literally, "you'll see what you want to see."

Suppose two playwrights, Lena and Gus, are asked to base a play on a real-life family they observe having Friday night dinner. Same family. Same dinner. Same circumstances. It's almost certain that when Lena and Gus sit down to write, the two plays will end up being *very* different. Vision makes you write about life the way you see it; therefore, one playwright might *emphasize* certain things which another playwright might miss altogether. Lena, who tends to *see* human relationships in a more positive light, might emphasize the bonds between the family eating dinner. Gus, on the other hand, whose vision is much more negative, might *emphasize* the rifts in the family. And they'd both be right! It's what they *see;* it's the aspect of the family they choose to *emphasize;* it's their *vision.* Objective reality is so complicated, plastic, porous, and faceted, it easily supports any given number of visions.

Of course, vision is much more complex than simply being positive or negative. Suppose Lena is a politically active feminist; she's sensitive to what she perceives as subtle sexism at the table. She sees that the mother and daughter set the table, bring in the food, and clear away the dishes. She notices the wife never contradicts the husband, even when it seems the wife would like to disagree. Together with her positive outlook, Lena's feminism is part of her vision. Gus had a troubled childhood; he's particularly sensitive to an undercurrent of alienation between the father and the teenage son. He sees the father ask the son several friendly little questions which the son either ignores or pretends not to hear. He watches the son leave the table before dessert, go into his room, and turn on his stereo full volume, playing music the father hates.

Already you can see two different plays forming, with two very different *emphases.* Because, although there is one family, one dinner, one set of circumstances, there are *two* visions *interpreting* "what actually happened." You're not a camera, recording life in all its detail; you're a person, with biases, prejudices, and emotions, who consciously and unconsciously selects and emphasizes those details that conform to your vision, your point of view.

As playwright, you want an audience to *share your vision,* to share your unique and special way of seeing things. That's why you write, so other people can feel as strongly as you feel about some person, some place, some event you thought was important enough to write about. And there's no better place than theater, with its immediacy and great vitality, to share your vision, to make your vision real for others.

Defining your vision takes time, perhaps a lifetime. (If the critics get hold of your work, more than a lifetime! Just ask poor Mr. Shakespeare.) But, before you get into any serious writing, it's very helpful to have a general sense of your vision, to know what you're trying to say when you sit down to write. Begin by trying the following:

Think about your favorite playwright. Ever notice how when you read or watch even a snippet from his or her work, you know immediately who the playwright is? You can virtually "see" the playwright behind every line, every character, every setting, every situation. ("Oh, that's a Pinter line!" "That monologue must be from one of Tina Howe's plays!" "He must be a Saroyan character!") What you're "seeing" is the playwright's vision; the playwright saying "this is how the world looks to me." Go back to the plays you know of your favorite playwright and try to define his or her vision: Is it bleak? Is it positive? Is it ironic? Is it political? Apolitical? Apocalyptic? Quixotic? Misanthropic? Humane? Ask questions. Find common threads that run through all the playwright's work. Try to be as specific as possible.

For example, you might begin to describe Chekhov's vision thus: "People must be productive to be truly happy. People should appreciate and encourage beauty. People must strive for a greater good, a better world. Any kind of waste—wasted lives, wasted resources, wasted beauty—is bad." Look at any Chekhov play and you'll see these four interrelated aspects of Chekhov's vision permeating each scene, each character, each relationship, each line, each gesture. And, if you read a biography of Chekhov's life, you'll see how Chekhov's vision grew out of his life experience.

Once you have defined your favorite playwright's vision as best you can, use the same approach to begin defining your vision. Take all the work you have done in the first two workshops. Find what common threads run through the scenes, the character sketches, and the other exercises you have worked on. What words and phrases best describe your vision? Spend some time just walking, thinking about your vision. (Now is the time to live your romantic "vision" of the writer to the hilt.) Look back over your life and jot down the major influences in your life: The people you have known. The books you have read. The conversations you have had. The ideas that have been passed on to you. The events you have been part of. The places you have lived in. Take voluminous notes. Look for patterns. Find the roots of your vision. Continue to add to and refine the "definition" of your vision as you look back over your life. Toward the end of your explorations, try to distill that definition down to a few lines.

> *Vision Exercise:* Define your vision in a succinct statement.

Think about what you have written and what you plan to write. How does your work reflect your vision? How can it reflect it better?

Exploring Raw Material for Your Play

Now that you have a fairly good idea of what your vision is—what you want to say—you can start thinking about what your play is going to be about. Because you'll be basing your play on your own experiences, the best way to begin the process is by looking back over your life for a time of your life with which you still have a strong emotional connection. What will clue you in to those times are often physical sensations: Does remembering still make you feel a tightness at the back of your throat? A twinge in the pit of your stomach? You'll find that a lingering, strong emotional connection with a time from your past usually centers on a still volatile or unsettling *relationship* (with one person, several people, a group of people) from your past. The best past relationships to use in plays contain the following elements:

—The relationship is, in some way, *unresolved.* (The hallmark of an unresolved relationship: Thinking about the relationship still troubles you; there are still questions in your mind that have never been answered satisfactorily.)

—The relationship was *crucial in shaping your vision.*

—A series of "dramatic" incidents occurred where the *conflicts* inherent in the relationship *came to a head.*

These interrelated aspects of a past relationship form the bedrock of good playwriting. Why?

As the adjective implies, an *unresolved* relationship creates *conflict*—the attempt to work out, or resolve, an imperfect relationship. How many times do we wish we could go back and undo something in the past? The marriage that fell apart. The rift that developed between two friends over the dumbest thing. As one of the characters in Chekhov's *The Three Sisters* laments: "I often wonder: what if you were allowed to begin life over again, this time consciously? If one life was just the rough draft, so to speak, and the other the final copy!" Playwriting allows you to treat your life as "a rough draft" for your play; in fictionalizing the experience, you can explore, understand, and even possibly resolve—at least on paper and onstage—what has remained unresolved. (Remember from "Harnessing the Power of the Unresolved Relationship" in the Intermediate Workshop how powerful an unresolved conflict can be? Unlike the characters in "Harnessing the Power of the Unresolved Relationship," you won't necessarily be trying to resolve the conflict in the present. You'll be going back to the original conflict, recreating and reliving it—an even more powerful experience.)

If you have had the chance to begin reading playwrights' biographies, you have probably seen how often writers, especially in their more autobiographical plays, use their writing as a means of getting to the root of, working through, and if not resolving, at least gaining perspective on an unresolved relationship.

What about the second aspect of a relationship that makes for good playwriting—*a relationship which was crucial in shaping your vision?* A playwright wants to share his or her vision with the audience. What better way to have the audience share in your vision than to take them with you through the events, incidents, and situations that were milestones in the development of your vision?

Suppose, for instance, an important part of your vision is that people who deny their creative instincts end up frustrated and unhappy. What better subject for a play than the root of your vision: your father who gave up a career as a jazz saxophonist to pursue more lucrative enterprises . . . who ended up frustrated and unhappy . . . who ended up taking it out on his relationships with his family and friends?

Also, because the relationship *shaped* your vision, it was a time of *learning,* a time of *conflict,* a time of *change*—all essential elements of good playwriting. All very well and good you're probably thinking, but how am I ever going to dig out of my past an unresolved relationship that was crucial in shaping or reinforcing my vision? Simple.

After having thought about your vision, you should have a fairly extensive list of past relationships that had some bearing on your vision. From that list, find a particularly powerful unresolved relationship to base your play on; not only relationships you lived through, but relationships you observed—as long as you were able to observe the relationship close up. (*The Glass Menagerie* is drawn from Williams' own troubled relationship with his mother and sister; *A Doll's House,* on the other hand, came out of Ibsen's acute insights into the stormy relationship of an intimate friend and her husband.) You'll probably be surprised by how many unresolved relationships from your life have shaped your vision.

The third aspect of a relationship that makes for good playwriting, *a series of "dramatic" incidents that occurred where the conflict(s) inherent in the relationship came to a head,* is the aspect most new playwrights neglect—and get in trouble for neglecting. A play, especially a full-length play, needs a *story*—a progression of interrelated incidents an audience can follow. New playwrights often think they can get by with interesting characters and relationships. Interesting characters and interesting relationships only work within the context of an interesting, compelling *story*.

You know your raw material has a good story to mine when you think back to relationships in terms of "I remember *what happened*" instead of "I remember *so-and-so*" or "I remember *such-and-such a place.*" The specific incidents connected with the unresolved relationship that shaped your vision should be highly charged, emotional—"dramatic." What is "dramatic"? Head-on confrontations. Clashes. Opposing forces in collision. Drama is *conflict*. Drama is intense interaction, building, building, building. Avoid raw material that will lapse into so much soul-searching, reminiscing, sitting around talking, and "rapping." Beware of relationships and situations where the people are uncommunicative and isolated. Of course, as you're building your play out of your life's raw material, you probably will want to beef up the story, changing or inventing incidents where necessary. But give yourself a fair start by finding a past relationship with a compelling story built in.

Here's an old adage that may prove helpful: "Most successful plays are either about love or power—or both." Why? Because both love and power are primal, have conflict built in, and are therefore compelling. Mull it over. Apply the adage to the plays you like—does it fit? Does the story of the raw material you're planning to use revolve around love and/or power?

Choose the relationship you're going to use for raw material carefully; you'll be living with (and reliving) this segment of your life for the next couple of months. Are you happy with what you have found? A little nervous? Good. Let's begin.

Start by exploring the raw material of your unresolved relationship, using the techniques you learned in the Beginning

Workshop. Map out the story, the sequence of incidents, the high points of the relationship when the conflict(s) inherent in the relationship came to a head. (If the high points/incidents are spaced over a long period of time, map them all out. You can always change the time sequence later, cutting, combining, and compressing incidents where necessary.) Under the headings "Setting," "Character," "Physical Activity," "Language," and "Conflict," list everything you can remember about each high point/incident of the past relationship you're dramatizing. For example:

—*Setting:* Was it night? Twilight? Was it chilly? Were we sitting on the porch steps? On the swing? Were we worried about the floorboards creaking?

—*Character:* What was he wearing? What was I wearing? What was I like back then? Did he used to laugh at his own dumb jokes? Why were we never able to make eye contact without giggling?

—*Physical Activity:* When she started to get nervous, didn't she doodle on her napkin? On the tablecloth? With a pen? With her eyebrow pencil?

—*Language:* What expression was it he always used when he did something foolish? Why did I mumble so much that night? (Was I cold? Scared?) Why did we keep talking at the same time? Weren't there lots of times when neither of us said anything? What was it about the way he talked I found so soothing?

—*Conflict:* What did she want? What did I want? What did she do to get her way? How did I try to stop her? Was it really an accident when she spilled her drink on me?

Review the lists periodically; maybe a detail on the list will trigger your memory of other details. Exploration is probably the most important step in the playwriting process. The downfall of most beginning writers comes from rushing through the exploration of their raw material in order to "start writing." Exploration *is* writing: Behind every wonderfully drawn character, every perfectly shaped scene, every exquisitely wrought speech lie layer upon layer of exploration. Have a thorough and objective knowledge of the raw material you're basing your play on. Exploring the raw material, understanding the raw material, is the whole foundation of your play. The relationship of successful playwriting and thorough exploration can't be overemphasized.

Chances are, as you explore, you'll find enough material for an 8-hour *Nicholas Nickleby*. Good. Better too much than too little. As you go through the process, you'll be *selecting* the details that work best for your play. You may also find that the particular past relationship you have chosen to dramatize takes place over a long period of time. Don't worry: Once again, as you go along, you'll play around with time, *compressing* the time scheme, the incidents, if necessary. Compression of events will "heat up" the drama in your play, much like a pressure cooker compressing steam. Writing a play in scenes instead of acts gives you a lot more freedom to play around with time.

In many ways, a playwright is very much an editor, *selecting and compressing* details and moments from life. (More about selection and compression later, when you begin working on your scenario.) But for now, accumulate vivid, telling details, as many as you can. Don't start to limit "what your play is about" too quickly. The play may end up being something very different from what you originally intended. Experienced playwrights find that happens constantly; it's a good thing. As you explore the raw material, you'll probably find several different ways to approach the play—in fact, you may find several different plays! Fine. For now, keep yourself open to all possibilities.

Jot down details; jot down ideas, thoughts, observations, insights on those details. Review the lists you make. Start looking for patterns. How did conflicts develop? How were they resolved? Were they resolved? Was there a central conflict? Who were the central "characters"? What characters were relatively unimportant? Of some importance? What rituals, major and minor, do you remember? Were any of them disrupted? How? Why? Was there a central ritual that defined the relationship(s) of the characters? Dig and think and dig and think until you can't dig or think anymore. Then dig and think some more. In fact, you should be exploring the raw material right up to the last line of the final draft of your play.

Storyline Exercise: Map out and explore the high points/incidents surrounding a volatile/unsettling past relationship for material for your play.

Establishing the Play's Premise

When you have explored your raw material enough that you feel the need to have some direction, begin pulling your material together by turning your vision into a *premise.* A premise is, to use the dictionary definition, "a proposition upon which an argument is based." You have a vision you want to share with an audience, right? Your vision is the *proposition;* your play is the *argument.* Your play fleshes out your vision, winning an audience over. In a well-put-together play, everything—every scene, every setting, every character, every line, every gesture—should be supporting your proposition, trying to win your audience over. You only have an hour or two onstage to "strut your stuff"; there's no room for fat in a play. So, once you figure out your premise, you can begin to focus your raw material, to select details that best flesh out your premise.

Consider, for instance, *A Doll's House.*

Central to Ibsen's *vision* is the belief in absolute honesty. To Ibsen, absolute, uncompromising honesty is the key to the emancipation of the human spirit. In *A Doll's House,* Ibsen turns his vision into a premise, a proposition that the play eloquently argues: "People cannot have true relationships until they learn to face themselves, be honest with themselves, and stand on their own." Reread the play carefully; notice how everything in the play supports Ibsen's premise. Of course, Nora, the central character, embodies Ibsen's premise. The audience watches her *learn* to face herself, *learn* to stand on her own. Nora's education is the thrust of the play. But what about, say, Mrs. Linde? How does she support Ibsen's premise? Mrs. Linde has had to learn to stand on her own, no easy task, but now she can fully appreciate herself, her life, and her new "honest" relationship with Krogstad. She is what Nora could become—not perfect perhaps, but a complete human being. Mrs. Linde also, to a great extent, encourages Nora's education.

What about the setting? How does it support Ibsen's premise? As you probably remember from "Creating Settings that Reflect the Conflict" in the Intermediate Workshop, Nora's home is cute, doll-like, charming, and inviting as the play opens, but more confining, more alien to Nora as the play goes on and Nora begins to grow up. The setting subtly underscores Nora's education. What about the scene where Nora rehearses dancing the tarantella for the party? It shows Nora beginning to change when Torvald expects Nora to be submissive to his instructions, but she isn't. She's beginning to show signs of independence, and even though independence scares her, it thrills her too. Look high, look low. Look hard. You'll find *every* element in *A Doll's House* argues Ibsen's premise.

If you wrote a play about the ex–jazz saxophonist described earlier, your premise would be: "People who constantly deny their creative instincts ultimately end up frustrated and unhappy." Everything in the play would argue for your premise. The jazz saxophonist would embody the premise. Perhaps another character would be someone who didn't deny his creative instincts and is reasonably happy and content.

Why a premise? Why not just sit down, write the play, and see what develops? The premise serves many purposes: It keeps the play in focus—no wandering plot, no extraneous elements. It *unifies* the play—just as large group scenes are more successful when they revolve around a central reflector, a play is more successful when all its elements revolve around a clearly defined premise. It gives the play a *forward thrust* as the audience watches the premise being stated, argued, and concluded. It provides *conflict*—built into the proposition of a premise is change, and with change comes conflict. And it's not as if you have to pull a premise out of the clear blue sky and force it on your raw material. The premise is there in your raw material; sometimes obvious, sometimes latent; the idea behind defining the premise is that when you know that the premise is there, you have a powerful tool at your disposal.

For now, spend some time thinking how your vision relates to the raw material you're exploring. Develop a succinct premise, a proposition that your play will argue, that will focus and unify your play as well as providing conflict and a forward thrust.

Premise Exercise: Define the premise of your play.

Write down the premise on a little piece of paper, and keep it in your pocket. Constantly weigh the raw material you have found (and are still finding) against the premise. ("Will this character's presence support my premise? What about this setting? This specific incident? This minor relationship?") Your premise helps you select details: What details might you want to emphasize? What details might you want to play down? What details seem to have no importance at all? (But don't throw anything away! Remember what you learned in the Beginning Workshop: What may not seem important now might be just what you need later.) You might revise your lists of details from time to time as your ideas about what the play is, where it's going, and what it needs to get there become increasingly clear.

Selecting and Compressing the Play's Raw Material

Playwriting is essentially a process of *selection and compression*—editing, shaping, and focusing your raw material into a finished work that boldly and succinctly argues and dramatizes your premise.

You know that you have only a very short time to win over your audience. Your play must be trim, powerful, and to the point. You have already begun the process of *selection,* choosing those details from your raw materials that best illuminate your premise. Compression aids selection in streamlining and focusing your play. In real life, interesting and complex relationships rarely develop over a short period of time. But a theater audience will often get lost in a story that spans many years; the conflict will become diffuse. Plays with sprawling novel-like structures rarely are successful onstage; unless the playwright is particularly skillful, the plays often lose their impetus, their forward thrust. "Compressing" the highlights of an unresolved relationship that may have occurred over several years into, say, a two-week period trims and focuses the story. Audiences love one crisis after another, one high point coming right on top of the last, compressed into a short period of time. Film can be laconic or sprawling; plays usually can't. Look at your favorite plays, at how much "action" the playwright packs into a brief time; much more seems to happen than would happen in real life. That's theater, and in the theater that much time compression seems real.

Think about *A Doll's House,* for example, and how different, how much less exciting, it would be if it happened over a longer period of time. Ibsen has *selected* the highlights of Nora's story, *compressing* them into one volatile, gripping *sequence* of incidents that takes place over the Christmas holidays. Compressing the time sequence of the play requires a great deal of ingenuity and craft, which is one reason you'll be writing your first full-length in scenes instead of acts. Writing in scenes allows you to worry a little less about how the highlights of your story flow together when the time sequence is compressed; you don't become obsessed with getting characters on or off stage realistically so a new scene can begin. A new scene can take place a few minutes, a few hours, or a few days later, instead of immediately.

Not only can the story and the time sequence of a play be compressed, but so can other elements—character, for example. Often, looking through your raw material and selecting only those characters who illuminate your premise, you'll find you have too many people for your play. In a first play especially, you want to keep down the number of characters, just so you don't have to play traffic cop. But one minor character, Leon, does one important thing, whereas another minor character, Gary, does another important thing. So you need them both—at least you need what both do. Compress them into one character, Chris, who does *two* things essential to the play.

Incidents too can be compressed. Suppose you have two brief incidents involving the same three characters. In the first incident, X happened. In the second incident, Y happened. Why not put together a new incident in which both X and Y happen? Not only is this more efficient, more economical, but with X and Y going on together, there's more going on, more variety, making the scene more exciting. The variations on this are limitless. For instance, in one incident, two sisters, Beth and Joanne, have a foul-mouthed, knock-down, drag-out fight over a man they both love. In the second incident, Beth and Joanne are having finger sandwiches with their very prim, rather prudish Aunt Eunice, whom they want very much to impress; the bulk of her estate goes to them. Put the two incidents together and . . . The possibilities are wonderful.

"Compressing that whole time of my life into a week? Making up new characters? New incidents? But then that's not what really happened!" You're right. It's not. And that's fine.

"What really happened" is the *basis* and *inspiration*—the raw material for your play. The play is your interpretation of "the real thing." You don't have to be 100 percent faithful to the incidents that inspired your play. After all, you're writing a plt a documentary. As playwright, you have the freedom to select, compress, manipulate, even invent new characters and incidents, if necessary.

While exploring your raw material, you have probably found many incidents that you'd like to include in your play. Even if the central events of the unresolved relationship you're using as raw material took place over a two-day period, there's that intense conversation Beth and Randy had at the breakfast table, Beth's argument with Grace just before you were supposed to go to town, and so on. Chances are there'll be incidents you'll have to make up when you didn't actually observe what happened. ("What did the three of them talk about on the porch? I know it was important, because all of a sudden Beth and Grace were acting civil toward each other again. . . .")

So here you are with a stack of juicy incidents ready to be turned into drama. So now you play editor. *Select:* "Does this incident illuminate my premise? Does this incident say pretty much what this incident says much better?" *Compress:* "The talk about all the garbage that went on back at Duke that I had with Beth and Grace was pretty much like the talk I had with Randy and Jack. If I put all five characters together, talking about that time at Duke, I'd save a scene. . . . And the five of them together, wow, that'd really add some fuel to the fire."

> *Compression Exercise:* Begin to think about selecting and compressing your raw material into the elements of a taut, lean, compelling play.

At this point, take notes only about possible deletions, modifications, and additions. Save the actual selection and compression for the scenario you'll be putting together in the next two steps of the workshop.

Putting Together a Rough Scenario

When you're well along in selecting and compressing incidents, begin to *arrange.* So that you begin to think in terms of "play" instead of "reality," let's call each incident a "scene." (Some scenes may be very long, some may be very short—don't worry about that for now; later you'll find that having scenes of various lengths is very much to your advantage.) When you arrange the scenes, you organize them, putting them in some sort of sequence (or order), a *story* an audience can follow—with a beginning, a middle, and an end. Let's call the entire sequence of scenes the framework or the *arc* of the play. You'll be revising the arc of your play right up to the final draft—making the story more compelling, more *dramatic*—but developing the arc begins with the scenario.

You have been working with a scenario since the Beginning Workshop. Because a full-length play is a much more ambitious undertaking than a scene, you'll be creating your scenario in two steps:

1. A "rough" scenario, so you can get some idea of where your play is going without having to worry about unimportant details;
2. A "detailed" scenario, which allows you to rework and refine what you sketched out in the rough scenario.

The rough scenario will have the following components: a working title; a brief description of the major and minor characters; a brief description of the major and minor relationships; a brief description of the major and minor conflicts; and a list outlining the arrangement of the scenes, from the first scene to the last, with a brief description of each scene. Each component of a rough scenario is described in detail below.

Developing a Working Title

Giving your play a title before you have written a line of dialogue may strike you as a bit absurd; however, especially for a full-length play, you'll find a "working title" invaluable. A carefully chosen working title, based on a thorough understanding of your raw material and premise, will give you an overall *feel* for both the *tone* and *content* of your play. Use the working title to give you a sense of direction, a sense of where your play is going. As you work through your play, you may, from time to time, lose sight of what you're writing about. A glance at a good working title will help you to say, "Yes, that's the play I'm working on." Think about the titles of your favorite plays. How do they reflect the play's content? The play's premise?

Title Exercise: Develop a working title for your play.

Remember, working titles are not set in concrete. As you learn new things about your play, the working title may be changed or altered accordingly. (If you have been reading the biographies of master playwrights, you have probably come across sections that describe the working process of the playwright. Usually, in those sections, you'll find some mention of the working titles the playwrights developed for their major works. Eugene O'Neill, for example, considered the following titles as he explored and drafted *Long Day's Journey Into Night: Diary of a Day's Journey, The Long Day's Insurrection, Retirement, Retreat, Vista,* and *Anniversary.* All are appropriate; each reflects what O'Neill thought was central to the play when he was at a particular stage in the play's development.)

Putting Together a Brief Description of the Characters

Look at the list of character details you compiled. Write a short, vivid description of each character in the play. The following information should be included: the name of the character, the character's age, a brief physical description, the relationship of the character to other characters in the play, and a one- or two-line history/profile of the character.

If at all possible, your play should have a strong *central character*—a character you will be emphasizing, a character "who the play is about," a character who best illuminates the central premise. This character should be someone with whom the audience can emotionally identify (or at least sympathize). By living vicariously through the central character, the audience learns what the central character learns as he or she travels through the arc of the play. Thus the audience gains an *emotional understanding of your premise,* which has much more impact than an intellectual appreciation of your premise. In *A Doll's House,* for example, Ibsen encourages the audience to identify—or, at least, side—with Nora. As Nora learns and grows over the arc of the play, the audience is in there with her, learning and growing too. By the end of the play, the audience has gained an emotional, not just an intellectual, understanding of Ibsen's premise.

Other examples of strong central characters include Heidi in *The Heidi Chronicles,* and Blanche in *A Streetcar Named Desire.* You can probably name a hundred plays that don't have one central character. Often the emphasis is split between two characters, several characters, even a group of characters (e.g., the plays of Chekhov). But for now, at this point in your career, you'll find your task much easier if you give yourself a strong central character to build your play around. You'll have a lifetime to experiment with other approaches after this workshop.

Determine whether the other characters in your play are *major, minor,* or *incidental.* Think about why and *if* each character is necessary to the play. If any characters—especially incidental characters—can be deleted or combined, do it. Economy should always be the playwright's watchword.

Character Exercise: Write a brief description of each character in your play. Determine whether the character is a central character, or a major, minor, or incidental character.

Putting Together a Brief Description of Conflict(s)

Determine first the central conflict, the one conflict that carries through the entire play (e.g., the struggle between Blanche and Stanley in *A Streetcar Named Desire*). How does the central conflict reflect your premise? How does it involve the central character? The other major and minor characters? What secondary conflicts, if any, are generated by the central conflict?

Conflict Exercise: Write down the central conflict and secondary conflicts, if any, in your play.

Roughing Out the Order of the Scenes

This component of the rough scenario should be thought through carefully, especially if your play has many scenes. You want to select and arrange a sequence of scenes (i.e., incidents), creating an arc that will carry your audience efficiently and powerfully from the beginning to the end of your story. Most people are natural storytellers; to build the arc of the play, listen closely to your instincts. Besides, the raw material itself should have the story built-in; you just have to dig the story out of all the extraneous events occurring at the same time. If your arc is flawed, you can always rework it later. As you select and arrange the sequence of scenes, keep the following in mind: *Each scene should illuminate your premise.* As the audience moves from scene to scene, they should be watching the development—the "arguing" (or dramatization)—of the proposition of your premise (which, of course, is connected with the central conflict and the growth of your central character).

Most new playwrights want to know: "Where do I begin my arc? Where do I start my play? What should the first incident be?" Again, trust your instincts, but keep in mind that you don't want to start the *story* so far from the heart of what you have to say that the play and the audience run out of steam before you get where you want to go. (A rule of thumb: The first scene should set up or establish the central conflict. A successful first scene should make the audience eager to know what's happening, what's going to happen—"Do you think they'll lose the farm? . . ." "If he keeps doing that, he's going to lose her, I know he is.")

Writing in scenes gives you more freedom to play around with the time scheme. But remember: the tighter the time scheme, the more you compress the arc, the tauter and more compelling the play will be. What may seem somewhat contrived on paper will probably prove exciting onstage. Because it's been a convention used by playwrights for centuries, fairly radical time compression makes perfect sense to a theater audience. In fact, think of when you're an audience. Don't you love it when one thing happens right on top of the other? Really gets your pulse rate up. Again, you're creating a play, not depicting reality detail for detail. You have all the license you want to twist, mold, and kick around reality to make a better, more *dramatic* play.

Progression Exercise: Rough out the order of the scenes —"incidents"—in your play.

Does the progression of scenes make sense? Does the story move logically and efficiently from one scene to the next? Any gaps? Any scenes too similar, too redundant? Can you see an arc? Is your premise stated and developed and brought to some sort of conclusion? Does your central character grow? Is the major conflict advanced? If everything isn't exactly what you want, that's fine. This is just the rough scenario. You'll be working and reworking the material through another scenario and several drafts. You'll have lots of time to explore and change. Right now, you just want a good bare-bones outline . . . a beginning. You want a sense of the play as a whole.

Sketching in the Individual Scenes

Once you have established a rough progression of scenes, sketch in each scene as follows:

—A line or two about the setting in the scene. (You may have every scene taking place in the same setting. You may have as many settings as you have scenes. Just get a flavor of each setting you plan to use: place, time of year, time of day.)

—A list of the characters involved in the scene

—A paragraph about what happens in the scene

—A line about how the scene advances the story

—A line about how the scene reveals the growth of the central character.

—A line about how the scene argues and develops the proposition you made in your premise.

Scene Exercise: Beginning with the first scene and working through to the last scene, sketch in each of the scenes in the play.

When you have finished sketching out the play, you should have a fairly good sense of where the play is heading. Before putting all the parts of the scenario together, ask yourself one more time: "Is this a taut, exciting, forward-moving *dramatic* situation?" Quite simply, ask yourself: "Is this a good *story?*" Remember: Even more than in fiction, story is crucial to the success of a play. If you find any weak or extraneous elements, go back, delete, modify, or add. If a scene looks like it's just sitting there, but the scene is crucial to the story, invent circumstances that give the scene punch.

Scenario Exercise: Put together all the parts of your rough scenario. Check for consistency and logic.

Before beginning the detailed scenario, look back over the rough scenario. Troubleshoot for major problems: entire scenes that don't advance the story or argue your premise, characters who seem extraneous, large gaps in the story, major inconsistencies. Make any necessary adjustments, deletions, or additions. If you're not sure about deleting a scene or a character, don't. Better to have too much to work with than too little; you can always cut problem scenes or extraneous characters later. If you feel you have to invent a scene to move the story along, or clarify a relationship, whatever, *do* it. Are you satisfied? Anxious to keep exploring? Then go on to the detailed scenario.

The Detailed Scenario

The detailed scenario fleshes out what you have started to put together in the rough scenario. By the time you complete your detailed scenario, you should have a sound understanding of every element of your play: You'll have a fairly good idea of whether the arc of the play—the sequence of incidents—hangs together. You'll understand your characters—not only their personalities and histories, but their specific motivations, goal(s), obstacles, and tactics throughout the play. You'll be aware of the dramatic possibilities in each setting. Of course, when you have finished the detailed scenario, your play is far from set. Drafting and polishing the dialogue, you'll continue reworking, revising, and rearranging every element of the play. But you should know your play intimately before you begin writing any dialogue.

In the following set of exercises, you'll be using tools and techniques you acquired in the Beginning and Intermediate Workshops to work through each scene slowly and carefully, so you can fully mine the dramatic possibilities in the scenes—and the play as a whole.

Just as you did when creating your scenario in the Beginning Workshop, you'll be describing in detail everything that happens in the scene, from lights up to lights down. Think in terms of action. Think in terms of conflict. Thinking of each scene as a step in the central conflict, determine the characters' goals, motivations, obstacles, and tactics. Does every element of the conflict relate in some way to the central conflict? Do you make full use of all the elements to dramatize the conflict: setting, character, physical activity, language? Can any of the motivations, goals, tactics, or obstacles be made more clear? More precise? Does the scene stray? Does it seem to lie flat in spots? Are the relationships consistent? Interesting? Honest? Does the story move forward? Does the outcome of the conflict in the scene make the whole play come closer to the outcome of the central conflict? Modify, replace, or delete any dead weight where the conflict lags.

When exploring the various elements in each scene, try to use every tool and technique you have worked with up to now. When exploring setting, for example, remember to ask all the questions you learned in the Beginning and Intermediate Workshops, such as: What time of day is it? What time of year? What's the weather like? What elements of the setting should be emphasized? Why are the characters in the environment? What activity or activities are the characters performing in the environment? Is the environment foreign or familiar to each of the characters? How does each character respond to the environment? How could elements of the environment be used as obstacles? As tactics? How does the setting reflect the conflict? Might another setting better reflect the conflict? Be thorough, not only with setting, but with every element, including character, language, and conflict.

As you explore the raw material from your past, use present observations and insights when helpful. Invent, when necessary. Feel free to experiment. Remember, there are no dead ends when you're playwriting. Each tangent, each detour you take, enriches your understanding of the direction you ultimately decide to take your play—or your play decides to take you. Spend as much time as you need exploring, working, and reworking everything in the rough scenario. If you feel your exploration of any element of the play is less than complete, go back and review what you learned in the previous two workshops. Hopefully, with the practice you gained doing scenarios for the exercises in the Intermediate Workshop, the tools and techniques of scenario making should be fairly instinctive at this point, so you shouldn't have to backtrack too much.

Detailed Scenario Exercise: Write down in narrative form—without dialogue—the moment-to-moment action in each scene of your play, beginning with the first scene and working through to the last.

When you're satisfied that you know all the elements of your play inside out, you can fine tune the detailed scenario.

Determining the Ritual Base of the Scenes and the Overall Play

Using "Understanding the Relationship of Ritual and Drama" in the Intermediate Workshop as a guide, find what kind of ritual each scene revolves around. Is it social? Family? Personal? Is the ritual disrupted? Do the rituals in all or most of the play relate to (or add up to) an overall *central ritual* that goes through the entire play? What is the central ritual (if there is one—and, more often than not, there should be one)? Is this central ritual disrupted? How is it disrupted? How do the rituals in each scene and the central ritual (if there is one) reflect your premise? Can any of the rituals be emphasized more? Can any one of them be more interesting? More in keeping with your premise and the central conflict? Make a list, briefly describing each ritual, scene by scene. Think about how the all the rituals relate to one another. Does a pattern evolve?

Ritual Exercise: Determine what ritual each scene in your play revolves around. Determine if your play has a central ritual that goes through the entire play and, if so, how the rituals in each scene relate to the central ritual. Modify the scenario where necessary.

Determining the Characters' Overall Goals

How does the central character's goal(s) in each scene he or she is in relate to his or her overall goal in the play? If you think of each scene involving the central character as a step toward the central character's achieving his or her overall goal, is there a natural progression from scene to scene? Do any scenes repeat steps unnecessarily? (If so, you might want to rethink the necessity of the scene.) If you list in order the central character's goals in each scene he or she is in, you should be able to see the arc of the play clearly delineated.

Try the same breakdown of overall goal and scene-by-scene goals for each of the major and minor characters. Each of the secondary characters' overall goals, as well as their scene-by-scene goals, should relate to the central character, either *complementing* or *opposing* the central character's goals. Opposing goals in collision give the play—and each scene—conflict. If a secondary character's goals do not complement or oppose the central character's goals, rethink the necessity of that character in a particular scene or in the play as a whole.

> *Goal Exercise:* Determine the overall goal and scene-by-scene goals for the central character and each of the major and minor characters. Determine and define complementary and opposing goals. Modify the scenario where necessary.

Giving the Sequence of Scenes Variety

The very last bit of fine-tuning can—and hopefully will—wreak havoc on your carefully and patiently wrought scenario. In the Beginning Workshop, you learned the importance of variety in a scene; you gave the characters a variety of tactics and obstacles to keep the conflict interesting and compelling. Variety is *critical* to a full-length play. An uninterrupted string of quiet scenes can lull an audience to sleep. A string of intense scenes can be too overwhelming for an audience. Too many two-character scenes in a row, and the audience's attention often will begin to wander. The same will happen with too many large-group scenes back-to-back. Or too many comic scenes, one after the other. Or too many "heavy" scenes. Or too many short scenes. Or too many long scenes. Or too many scenes that focus only on one character or one situation or one idea. Even if each scene in a sequence of identical scenes is perfectly formed, too much of a good thing onstage becomes relentless, and the audience, consciously or unconsciously, begins to say, "Enough already, enough!" Variety maintains an audience's interest by keeping it on its toes, never knowing what to expect next.

Variety not only breaks up the tedium; the contrast of two very different scenes can make one or both scenes much more powerful than if each scene stood alone. For example, amid all the action and pageantry in *Henry IV, Part I,* Shakespeare gives King Henry and Prince Hal a moment alone together when they talk to each other not as king and prince, but as father and son. The scene between the two men is simple, honest, intimate, stirring. The scene has even greater impact because it's preceded by a brief scene where the King and Prince are surrounded by the entire royal court. Shakespeare could have easily left out the court scene. But the contrast between the large-group scene and the two-character scene heightens the intimacy of the father-son talk much more than if the two-character scene stood alone. In other plays such as *Hamlet, King Lear,* and *Macbeth,* Shakespeare adds variety by placing comic scenes right in the middle of a progression of tragic scenes, which allows the audience a bit of a breather and, by contrast, heightens the intensity of the tragic scenes.

(As a role model for writing plays in scenes instead of acts, Shakespeare is unsurpassed. He wrote all his plays in scenes;

after Shakespeare's death, publishers of his plays arbitrarily lumped the scenes together into acts. Read his plays, see good productions of his plays—like the brilliant work the Royal Shakespeare Company brings to America.)

Look at how your scenes line up. Does your play need more variety? If so, you can use exercises from Intermediate Workshop to help you. Maybe four two-character confrontations in a row could be broken up by adding a third character to one of the two-character confrontations. Maybe a different central reflector would give two very similar large-group scenes more sense of contrast. Maybe three consecutive manic comic scenes might benefit from making one of the scenes a comic/serious scene—or a quiet scene. (Why do you think the lovers sing their duet or Harpo plays the harp in the middle of the mayhem of a Marx Brothers film?) Maybe a string of scenes revolving around the central character would benefit from a scene without the central character. The possibilities are limitless. If the time sequence of the play is not critical, juggling the order of the scenes a little might provide variety without disrupting the arc of the play. You may balk at the idea of straying from the specific incidents and time scheme of the original story, but that's a playwright's prerogative and duty: to select and compress and shape and edit and add to the raw material as necessary in order to create the best play possible.

You have probably spent a long time creating the detailed scenario. You're probably aching to start writing dialogue. Not yet. Take a break. Read the detailed scenario through several times, then put it aside. Spend a week or so doing something other than playwriting. Sit out on the fire escape and drink iced tea and catch up on all those back issues of *People* and *Atlantic Monthly* you haven't had a chance to read. Just try *not* to think about the play. Let all the work you have done sink into your subconscious without consciously helping it. Don't read any plays, or see any plays. Don't do anything to make you think about playwriting. And, whatever you do, don't talk about your play with anyone. For now, let what the play is about be your little secret; let your urgency to "tell it to the world" fuel your first draft.

After a week, maybe two, when you're feeling relaxed, ready and eager to continue, press on.

Writing an Exploratory First and Last Scene

Drafting the first *and* the last scene of the play before you draft the intermediate scenes may seem a bit bizarre, but it gives you a sense of where your play is coming from and where it's going. How does the play—the story, the characters—start out? How *might* the play—the story, the characters—end up? The success of this step depends on your attitude. You can't be too serious. Keep a light touch when adding dialogue and stage directions to the first and last scene. Don't treat what you write as a final product; it's just a little exploration, another step in discovering what your play is about. Done with the right attitude, drafting a preliminary first and last scene will make you a little less apprehensive about what's ahead. You'll realize it's not that long a road to travel from the beginning of the play to the end. You'll have a surer sense of the central conflict, the central ritual, your characters' overall goals. You'll hear most, if not all, of your characters talk for the first time. You'll be motivated to keep writing, to see what transpires between the first and the last scene. There'll be many changes of course, in both scenes, as you work and rework the play. The last scene in the final draft of the play may end up altogether different from your exploratory last scene. For that matter, so may the first scene. But at least you'll have a starting point, and a point to head to.

In the following exercise, you'll be using the tools and techniques you developed in the Beginning and Intermediate

Workshops to draft the dialogue and stage directions for the first and last scene in the play.

When doing the exercise, review the scenario for the first scene. Then put the scenario aside and try not to look at it again while you draft the dialogue and stage directions for the first scene. (The dialogue loses its spontaneity when you use the scenario as a "follow-the-dots." Let yourself be free to improvise a little. If you know your raw material inside out and have put together a good scenario, you'll feel all the more confident to take risks.) Review the scenario for the last scene. Then put it aside while you draft the dialogue and stage directions for the last scene.

Draft both scenes *one time only.* Don't rewrite. Looking at the two scenes, you probably see everything from minor inconsistencies to major problems. Fine. But *don't rewrite.* Take as many notes for later changes, additions, and deletions as you want, but don't change a line. Don't touch a stage direction. Don't try to put in that great moment you had in your scenario which you forgot to put in the scene. Don't try to smooth over that preposterous tangent the first scene suddenly took in mid-scene. There's a very good reason for not rewriting at this point: Until you have roughed out the whole play, you won't know what works and what doesn't work.

You might feel very insecure, hating what you have written. The writing might strike you as rough, raw, awkward, even embarrassing. Most beginning playwrights show their insecurity at the beginning of the play. They become too retentive. They don't improvise. They don't allow themselves to experiment. They don't take risks. They don't trust their creative instincts. Worst of all, they become mired in writing and rewriting and touching up and fixing the beginning of the play until they are so exasperated that they don't want to look at the play again. If they finally let go and finish the play, more often than not, they find all the picayune work they did on the beginning of the play was for nothing. The beginning may be reworked extensively, even cut completely. One reason for this exercise is, by having you work almost simultaneously with the first *and* last scene, you are forced to be aware that there is a whole play to be written, not just a first scene. Trust your instincts when you draft the two scenes; fly.

> *Dialogue Exercise:* Draft the dialogue and stage directions for the first and last scene of the play.

When you have roughed out the dialogue and stage directions for both the first and last scenes, consider the following:

—Can you get a better sense of the arc of the play?

—Do you have a better understanding of the direction of the central conflict? Of the central ritual? The overall goals of some of the characters?

—Does the tone of the two scenes seem fairly consistent? (Do both scenes belong to the same play?)

—Do either or both scenes stray from the scenario? How? Why?

—Do your characters talk for themselves? Are you delighted to finally have them talking? If not, why not?

Ask yourself these questions. Think about them. Take extensive notes, but *do not* rewrite either scene. Use the insights you have gained on the next step of writing a full-length play: the first draft.

Writing the First Draft of Your Play

The directions are simple enough. Keeping in mind what was said in the last step, you are now going to work through the play, scene-by-scene, beginning with Scene Two. Briefly review the scenario for Scene Two, then put it aside. Draft the dialogue and stage directions for Scene Two. Briefly review the scenario for Scene Three, then put it aside. Draft the dialogue and stage directions for Scene Three, until you have worked your way through the whole play. Take notes on changes, additions, and deletions you think may be necessary. But *don't rewrite,* not a line, not until you have finished the entire first draft of the play. (Note: Because you're creating an arc, you may feel the play has changed enough by the end to warrant a new last scene, different from the exploratory last scene you wrote in the previous exercise. Fine. Write it.)

You should write the first draft as swiftly, deftly, and efficiently as possible. Don't be sloppy and careless, but, more important, don't succumb to the trap so many beginning playwrights fall victim to: Being a perfectionist, wanting a finished product the first time through. Your goal is to see a complete play sitting in front of you. *Not a perfect play,* just a complete play.

Paraphrasing what Anton Chekhov once advised a struggling writer: If you spend longer than a month on a first draft of a full-length play, you're spending too long. Let the need to tell your story drive you forward. If the first draft strays from your scenario, so what? That may be just the tangent your play needs. If the first draft doesn't seem to be "saying" what you want it to "say," so what? Maybe it's saying something else you didn't realize you want to say. If there are occasional outrageous inconsistencies in character, tone, or other elements of the play from scene to scene, terrific. Consistency will come in the rewrites. (And even then, you'll have to be careful not to mistake consistency for turning everything into homogenized milk!) Remember, nothing you write is set in concrete; anything and everything can be changed eventually. When writing, above all, *trust your instincts.* If you have explored your raw material thoroughly, and written your scenario carefully, your instincts should serve you just fine.

If you have the willpower, try not to read a scene you have written more than once or twice—and only immediately after you have finished drafting it. Take notes on possible changes, additions, and deletions. But don't dwell on what you preceive as the faults, inconsistencies, and lapses in the scene; look instead for what works in the scene. Be excited about what you're creating. Nagging doubts, frustrations, any bad feelings you harbor about scenes you have already drafted will color the scenes you still have to draft. Like the play, you should be moving forward. Start each scene fresh and enthusiastic. A good, loose attitude is all-important in approaching the first draft. You'll be surprised what a good job your subconscious will do all by itself, deciding what works and what doesn't, and planning the second draft of the play, without your consciously fussing, fretting, and moaning, driving yourself crazy with self-doubts. Once again: *Trust* your instincts, *trust* your creativity.

> *First Draft Exercise:* Write the first draft of your play, from Scene Two through to the end.

When you have finished the entire first draft, read it over several times, carefully and critically. Read it aloud (by yourself) at least once. Ask the questions you have learned to ask throughout the three workshops. Look for consistency and clarity. Look to see if the play "hangs together." Take notes, not so much on each scene but on the overall play. *Do not rewrite.*

"Why can't I rewrite now? I've just finished the first draft." Exactly. You have *just* finished. You need a little *perspective* on what you have done. So, lock your first draft and notes in the desk drawer, and take another week or so off. Relax; rejuvenate yourself; do unplaywrighty things. Discuss life with the sea lions at Sea World. But whatever you do, don't go near that play. Try not to think about the play. And don't talk about the play with anyone—or worse, show someone the first draft. It's a very delicate time, nurturing both the play and your ego from the first draft to rewriting and polishing the play; a simple, off-handed remark or piece of well-intentioned advice can undermine months and months of good work.

Later, when you're relaxed, when your head's clear and your

pulse isn't racing anymore, take the first draft out of the desk drawer.

Rewriting and Polishing Your Play

Most experienced playwrights write at least three drafts of a play before they begin submitting the play to theater groups or contests. The rewards of reworking and honing a play are many. With each successive rewrite, you become a little less overwhelmed by, a little more comfortable with, the "Frankenstein" you have created. You can troubleshoot technical problems more adroitly. You become more intimate with the characters and their story.

The three or so drafts you do before you send the play to theater groups or contests are just the beginning. As you'll read in the next part of the book, once the play gets to theater, once you start collaborating with actors, directors, designers, and dramaturges, you'll continue to rework and refine what you thought was perfect at your desk. That's what's awful and wonderful about theater. And a successful playwright is one who is flexible enough and secure enough to realize a play is never really finished. Some playwrights, in fact, like Tom Stoppard and Friedrich Durrenmatt, keep rewriting a play even after it has been produced and published. At the wishes of his director, Elia Kazan, Tennessee Williams completely reworked the third act of *Cat on a Hot Tin Roof* for its initial production in 1955. And he made further revisions to the third act for the Broadway revival of the play *some twenty years later!*

Before you send the script to theater groups or contests, rewrite the play as many times as you feel necessary. Realize, however, that if you're a true craftsperson, you'll never be completely satisfied. Keep a balanced perspective when you rewrite; be careful of two extremes. Beware of too much rewriting, of being too scrupulous, too self-deprecating. Very simply, you can write the life out of the script. An even greater danger for new playwrights is to be afraid to change a thing, to think that each word on the page is precious, golden, not to be touched. Avoid the "that's it; the play's done; it's perfect" attitude you were cautioned about earlier. Rarely do plays "work" after one draft. Even a seemingly effortless piece—such as one of Neil Simon's lighter comedies—is usually the product of painstaking draft after painstaking draft. As Neil Simon has said in interviews time and time again, his plays only look effortless after much, much perspiration, crumpling of paper, grinding of teeth, and banging his head against his desk.

You have plugged away diligently through three workshops. You know your work habits, your quirks, your needs—what works for you, what doesn't. How you rewrite and how many times you rewrite is up to you. Unlike the first draft, rewriting often takes a long time. You should maintain your energy and enthusiasm throughout the entire process. Take breaks between drafts to regain your perspective. You might even want to start a new project as you're putting the final touches on the play. That's fine; most experienced writers find that by overlapping their projects they fuel, not diminish, their creativity. What follows is a general guide for rewriting and polishing a full-length play. You should find it useful but, at this point in your development, you may want to modify it to your "style." Please feel free.

Revising and Polishing Your Play: A Guide

The most efficient and effective means of rewriting and polishing a full-length play is to alternate between two steps: (1) looking at the overall play, and (2) looking at the play scene by scene, in minute detail. Each method of approaching the play illuminates the other approach, making your work easier, more efficient, and much more fruitful than if you just focus on one or the other approach.

Read through the first draft—and notes you made on the first draft—several times. Think first in terms of the overall play. Think in terms of storyline. Think in terms of the play moving forward—logically, consistently, efficiently, with no holes and no extraneous elements. Work through the first draft as follows:

—Consider whether the play as a whole eloquently states and argues your premise. Are there any *major* elements that don't work toward stating or arguing your premise? Any scenes? Any characters? Any incidents? Even if a scene is well-written, or a character is beautifully drawn, if the scene or character is extraneous, it's *extraneous*. A major stumbling block of many beginning playwrights is the inability to cut elements in the play that work wonderfully by themselves but do not help the overall play. The best way to spot extraneous elements is to notice that they seem to literally float free from the forward movement of the play. Everything in the play comes to a halt. Now is the time to get rid of that character, scene, or bit of dialogue you always knew never belonged in the play, but you hated to let go. Close your eyes, grit your teeth, and cut mercilessly.

—Consider the various arcs in the play: the arc of the scenes, the arc of the central conflict, the arc of the central character, the arcs of the various major and minor characters. Does each arc seem tight? Does each arc develop *consistently*, *logically*, and *efficiently* from step to step, moving forward all the time? Does the progression of scenes move along logically? Efficiently? With variety? Are there any scenes missing? Any extraneous scenes? If you sketched out the arc of the central conflict, *it should literally follow an arc*: efficiently and logically building to some sort of ultimate confrontation, then falling away to some sort of resolution, however tenuous. Does the central conflict and your premise follow a similar arc, the building of the arc following the statement and argument of your proposition? What about the arc of the characters' growth? Do the characters develop consistently? Logically? Efficiently? Does the central character's arc and your premise follow a similar arc, the central character's growth following the statement and argument of your proposition?

—Briefly check the first draft against the scenario and your notes: Are any other *major* alterations suggested that still make sense at this point? Can you see why you sometimes might have strayed—why you had to stray—from the scenario?

After you have considered all of the above, start from the beginning and work through the play, making any necessary *major* changes, additions, or deletions that will improve the logic, consistency, and efficiency of the overall play. (Remember: If you delete or change, don't throw anything out; it may prove important, if not invaluable, later.) After you have completed reworking the major elements of the first draft, focus on the next step, on careful, detailed, scene-by-scene work.

Scene-by-scene rewriting and polishing require patient, detailed work, but don't be alarmed—you have done it all before. Essentially, you do for each scene in the play what you have been doing for each scene you have written since the end of the Beginning Workshop. Start with the first scene and work through the play. Using your scenario, the work you have done on the overall play, and any notes you have taken as a guide, consider the following:

—Is the premise apparent in each scene?

—Are the characters consistent within the scene? Do they speak for themselves?

—Is the conflict strong? Are the goals, motivations, obstacles, and tactics clear? Specific? Varied? Interesting? Are there any dead spots, where the scene does not seem to move forward? (Be careful: Some of the deadest spots in scenes are those brilliant little moments—very funny, very dramatic, perfect little gems—that have nothing to do with the scene or the play. Cut mercilessly anything that does not work *for* the scene. Use the same test you used earlier: Does the "brilliant little moment" just float free from the forward movement of the play? Cut, cut, cut! And save, in case you need whatever you have cut later.)

—Does the scene "hang together"? (Does it move logically from one moment to the next?)

—Can the scene begin later? End sooner? Is the meat of the incident only two pages out of the six you have written? Are you spelling everything out—every nuance of a relationship, every character detail, the entire history of a conflict? (Remember: Don't underestimate a theater audience. They don't need—or want—everything spelled out. You don't want to keep the audience in the dark until the point they become frustrated, but a little mystery draws them into the play. An audience with tantalizing questions they want resolved is an attentive audience. As you redraft and polish, and become more comfortable with the play, you'll find yourself more and more willing not to spell everything out. Hard to face up to, but true: It's not that most authors don't trust their audience; it's that they don't trust their material.)

—Is the setting used to full advantage? Does it subtly underscore the conflict? Could the scene work better in another setting? Do the characters use elements of the scene effectively as tactics or obstacles?

The preceding are just some of the key questions you can ask about each scene. Ask all the questions you have learned to ask throughout the three workshops. Make any minor changes, additions, or deletions you jotted down as you went through the first draft, which you still think are valid. Focus on trouble spots. Use everything at your disposal to find a clear, effective way of solving the problem. (Creativity is essentially *problem solving*. For instance, does a character keep using the same tactic until it becomes boring? How might you give variety to tactics that the character uses?) Cut any excess; get down to the heart of the conflict. Add, shape, modify, and invent when necessary. Aim for what you aimed for when working with the overall play: *consistency*, *logic*, *efficiency*.

When you have finished working through the play scene-by-scene, consider the overall play again. Make any major revisions suggested by your scene-by-scene work. Focus on *variety*, *emphasis*, and *balance*. Is there enough variety between the scenes? The characters? Are the elements—scenes, characters, ideas, and so on—you want emphasized, emphasized enough? Too much? Are the various elements in the play balanced? Within themselves? (For example, is the character "in the right" too good, to the point she's not believable?) Against each other? (Is there too much of one character, not enough of his or her antagonist to create a balanced conflict?) Make any changes, additions, or deletions.

Then, once again, look at the play scene-by-scene for variety, emphasis, and balance. Again, make any changes, additions, or deletions. You have now gone through the play twice—two times looking at the overall play, two times looking at the play scene-by-scene. If you want to repeat the two steps again, do. Just don't overdo it to the point where you become bored, frustrated, or begin to write the life out of the script.

Type the script out as you learned in "Writing a Scene" in the Beginning Workshop. When typing the script, begin each scene on a new page. Briefly describe the time and place of the scene at the beginning of the scene. Make act divisions, if you wish, wherever a break seems natural. (Or, do what Pinter does at the beginning of his play *Betrayal*: Suggest where an act break would be appropriate.) Type the script yourself —even if you can barely hunt and peck. A noted director types out every script she works on, even if it's been published in an acting version; she says it's amazing how much you learn about the play when you're typing it out, every word of the script going through your fingers. Carefully reread the typewritten script. Read it aloud, at least once. With the play laid out neatly before you, new changes and cuts will probably jump out at you. Strange how it always happens: You make the play presentable, ready to send out to theater groups or contests, and suddenly the insert you thought worked perfectly looks all wrong, and the cut you thought you had to make doesn't seem to work at all. Of course, when you're reading the typewritten script, maintain your perspective; don't be too hard (or too easy) on yourself. Make any necessary changes, additions, or deletions. And retype a clean copy. Consider it a labor of love.

Now that you have a second draft, have a reading of the play at your home, apartment, room, the student union—any informal, nonperformance space. Use the best actors you can find. If you took the advice in the Beginning Workshop seriously and have been trying to get involved in the local theater scene, you should be getting to know—or at least know the performances of—various actors. If you want certain actors to read key roles, and you don't know the actors personally, get in touch with them. Send them a copy of the script; tell them you'd like them to read such-and-such a role at your place on such-and-such a date. You'll be surprised how many will say yes, if their schedules allow. Invite theater artists you know—directors, designers, actors, your mentor (if you have one—and, at some point in your career you should have someone whose opinion you trust above all others)—and friends to listen and comment. Keep the evening—or afternoon—low key.

At the reading, listen carefully as the play is being read. Take notes on trouble spots. (If you're nervous, tape record the reading to play back at a time when your palms aren't so damp.) Keep an ear open to audience reaction: laughter (hoped for, unexpected, and unwanted), "you-can-hear-a-pin-drop" silence, coughing, shuffling, murmuring, mumbling, sighing . . . snoring. If you carefully feel out how your audience is reacting as the reading is happening, you can often learn more about your play than during the after-reading discussion.

That's why so many experienced playwrights stand at the back of the house during previews of their new plays: not so much to watch the play, but to get a feel for the audience watching the play. Take notes on what you observe.

After the reading, encourage discussion. Ask the group to be open and honest, not polite. Ask the actors and the audience specific questions. Let them give you as much feedback as possible. Ask them to be as specific as possible about their likes and dislikes. Don't get emotional; keep a poker face. And don't tell people what the play is about. Let them tell you. You learn much more by listening carefully and objectively than by being defensive or making excuses. Jot down or tape record what everyone has to say.

Think about the comments for a week or two. Allow yourself perspective—on both favorable and less faborable criticism, also on your own response to the reading. Did your feeling of what works and what doesn't work change because of the reading? Do a *third* draft of the play, incorporating what you learned from the reading and the discussion. Use the alternating overall/scene-by-scene approach described above to create the third draft, modifying the approach to best suit your needs. If you feel reasonably encouraged about the third draft, it's time to send the play out. To theaters. To workshop theater groups. To contests. Don't do what so many playwrights do and not send a play out until it's "perfect." Send your play out as soon as you can to as many people as possible. Get yourself known—locally, regionally, nationally. The second half of the book will guide you with advice on the how's, where's, and when's of getting your play produced.

A final word of advice: A writer writes. As you send out your first play to theater groups or contests you should be exploring a second play, maybe even jotting down ideas for a third. The only way to learn your craft is to practice your craft. Practice will allow you greater assurance, greater freedom, greater flexibility, and a greater ability to say what you want to say as a playwright. You just can't dream of that perfect play you're going to write someday—you must work; you must write. Perhaps you were dissatisfied with what you did with the first play. Good! Dissatisfaction propels a playwright through his or her career, trying to make the next play better than the last.

Use what you can from the three workshops. Reject, add to, or modify what you need to when you need to. If, for example, you want to move from scene-by-scene writing to writing in continuous acts, by all means *do*. Now that you have a good idea of how to create a sequence of scenes, you won't find it much more difficult to write with a tighter time sequence. You can feel more at ease to focus on the mechanics of getting characters on and off stage without disrupting the "flow" of the act. Maybe you have some ideas for creating a scenario that would work better for your purposes. Try it. Chances are you want to invent more: totally fictional incidents, totally fictional characters, perhaps dramatizing a unique incident you overheard someone talking about when you took the bus from Cairo to Peoria, fleshing out the incident with characters drawn from people you have known at various times in your life. . . .

Infinite possibilities. Unlimited choices. Unbridled freedom. All yours. Explore. Experiment. Play around with playwriting. Just as long as you're writing. A writer writes.

PART TWO

BEING A PLAYWRIGHT

CHAPTER FOUR

GETTING YOUR PLAY READ BY THE RIGHT PEOPLE

You have written a play. You were alone with your typewriter or computer while you wrote it, but now that it's finished, you're not going to be alone anymore. Unlike the novelist or short story writer, the playwright isn't allowed to keep an arm's length away from the business world. Like it or not, you're going to have to pursue people if you want your play performed. You have to get out and meet people who can stage your play. And after *that* is done, you're going to have to become a part of a collaborative experience and work with directors, actors, producers, and others.

Throughout the first half of the book, you were advised to attend plays—to see the works of the master playwrights and the works of contemporary writers as well. The playwright needs to be familiar with the language of the theater, with the literature and the traditions of the theater before he or she can successfully launch a playwriting career. By now, if you have been following the advice in the workshop session, you are familiar with more than one theater company in your area. You have attended a variety of plays and are perhaps even getting recognized by your local companies. (If nothing else, you're noticed by the box office staff who gratefully accept your cash for tickets to their productions!) Now it is time for you to start getting to know some of the other personnel at the theater or theaters you have been attending. You have finished a draft of your play and now you need to go to the theaters, both to see plays and meet actors, directors, and producers.

Start with the theater companies you have gotten to know. Whether they are college theaters, community theaters, semi-professional or professional companies, you must make the effort to identify yourself as more than just a member of the audience. Enjoying the theater is not enough. Playwrights must learn to study theater. You have to learn to sit through plays that are flawed and analyze why they aren't working. (The acting might be poor. The script falls apart in the second act. The director might have gotten in the way. Learn to figure out what makes this evening in the theater less than successful for you.) Watch workshops and showcases because you're interested in seeing a particular director's work or because there is an actor in the play who you think might be right for your script.

Being part of the theater profession means going to the theater to be supportive of other people's work. A great many noncommercial theaters will arrange complimentary tickets if they know that you are a playwright interested in observing their work. Again, introduce yourself to the box office people if you are interested in saving some money. They can often tell you if it is better to come on certain nights if you'd like comps (free tickets). When calling to make reservations, ask if the theater has a comp policy for professionals. The worst thing that can happen is they'll say no. But even if they do, many times they will mark right next to your name on the reservation sheet that you are a playwright and soon more than one person in the business will recognize you as a writer for the theater. Oftentimes, actors and directors ask to see the reservation list before a performance, because it gives them an idea of who is out there. So chances are very good that by the time you finally get up the courage to start introducing yourself, many of the theater company will already recognize your name and be curious about what kind of a playwright you are.

Once you start meeting people who work in the theater, don't be shy about showing off your work. You need to get people's impressions of your play. Actors are always looking for a new role or, better yet, for a good playwright to write a role for them. Start with the actors. Get to know them and if they ask to read one of your works, give them a copy. (And we stress a copy—never the original.) If you can't get an actor interested in reading your play, try a box office person. Most box offices are staffed by young would-be actors, directors, producers, or combinations of all three. These people are looking for projects to get involved in and will usually have the time to read an unknown playwright's work and also will get together to talk with you about it.

Once you have at least one person interested in your play, start planning the first step of the collaborative workshop process. Talk with that person about acting in a cold reading of the script if the person is an actor. If he or she is a director, see if the person would consider casting the reading of the play for you. If the person wants to be a producer, ask if he or she would like to take care of all of the details of the first public reading of your new play.

The Cold Reading

You have a draft of your play typed. Maybe new acquaintances you met at your local theater have read the play and have said they are interested in it. Maybe you haven't been able to get people at a theater to look at your play, but you still want to get started. So what do you do now? You should have a reading of the play.

There are two types of readings you can pursue—the cold

reading and the staged reading. The cold reading is an unrehearsed, unstaged reading done in a sit-down situation with a stage manager or director reading the stage directions as they come up in the script. The staged reading is a reading that is put on its feet by a director. The actors carry scripts, but move around the stage and carry out minimal blocking. A director usually has 15 to 20 hours of rehearsal before showing a staged reading.

If you don't have a director, or if you haven't already heard your play read out loud by others, a cold reading is best. You can organize it yourself by posting signs in a local college or theater, asking for actors and a stage manager and/or director. If you can audition the actors who call you, that's best. Let the actors see a copy of your script and make it clear to them what time you want them and where the cold reading will be held. It's best to hold a cold reading on a stage or in a classroom, but you can always have it in your apartment. Ask the actors to read the script ahead of time and have them come to the cold reading a half hour before the reading is to start. That way they can talk about any problems they might be having with the script.

As you're getting ready for your first reading of the play, keep letting other people read it. Feel free to submit the play to contests and producers (later on we give you lists of those addresses, submission guidelines, etc.). Playwriting is not like some other forms of writing where multiple submissions are considered wrong. You want numerous people reading your material and responding to it. A very important rule of playwriting is not to be shy about showing your work to other people. And once they have read the material, be gracious in accepting their comments. Generally you can assume if the person who has read your play has nothing to say about it, that it is best—if you want to maintain a relationship with that person—not to hound them for a response. If someone has nothing to say it means they either didn't care for the work or else they simply found nothing to connect with. If they do have something to say, then be polite and listen. You don't have to agree, but you should remain calm and listen to their comments, which might be made in person or in writing. If someone encourages you to show them more of your work, do just that. Most people in theater are professionals and they are not going to ask you to send more material if they are not interested in reading it. Conversely, if nothing is said about submitting anything more, you might think twice before sending another script.

Now back to getting the cold reading set up. The first reading of a play can be one of the most useful tools that a playwright has or it can be a total waste of time. The key as to what type of experience it will be lies in the actors and in the talents of the person who is helping to cast the reading. If you have been able to get a person who is interested in directing or producing to assist you with your first reading, let them suggest actors of proven abilities. Intelligent readers who are able to bring a sense of the play and of their characters to a cold reading are much more important than getting an actor who is the right physical type or the right age.

It is equally important that the playwright and the other workshop participants—including whatever audience will be invited—understand the limitations of the cold reading. The main purpose of a cold reading is for the playwright to hear his or her words. A cold reading should never be used as a backer's audition or as a tryout for a play. In recent years more and more commercial (i.e., profit-making rather than nonprofit) producing outlets have been relying on readings of scripts—often cold—to tell them whether the play is one they should take a gamble on and produce. Cold readings were never intended for this purpose. As we said earlier, keep sending your play out to be read and keep gathering responses and comments about your script, but consider the first reading—the cold reading—to be the first step in the collaborative developmental process. The idea behind a successful cold reading is that the playwright will be able to hear, often for the first time, the play read.

The first step of a cold reading is to schedule a time and room that is convenient. Cold readings are usually scheduled around performances to make it easier to get working actors involved either as readers or as audience members. This can occasionally be taken to extremes that are not helpful to the playwright or to any of the other participants. (The authors have attended cold readings at 10:00 A.M. on Sundays as well as at 2:00 A.M. on a Saturday morning. Both of these times presented problems before the reading itself could even be evaluated.) Most communities have Monday as their "dark" night for theater. A Monday evening thus becomes a logical time to schedule a cold reading. Midday cold readings are also worthwhile if the participants (and remember the audience is an important participant) are all either working for the same company and thus on the same schedule, or else if enough people can take time from their various jobs at this time of day to participate in the cold reading process.

Once the schedule of the reading has been set, casting should begin. Again, this is one of the most important aspects of the cold reading process. If the playwright is working with an existing workshop or theater company, chances are good he or she will have a pool of actors from which to select for the cold reading. These are actors who have proven themselves to be good readers, able to make sense of a script with just one prior read-through, and who are also reliable and will show up on time for the reading. Most cold readings that don't work use friends of the playwright in pivotal roles. If you are fortunate enough to be invited to participate in an ongoing workshop's cold reading series, trust them to provide you with good, dependable actors.

After casting has taken place, then it is the playwright's responsibility to make sure that good clean copies of the script are ready to be given out to the actors before the reading. An actor will read through a script at least once and spend time preparing, even for a cold reading, if the playwright is conscientious and has legible scripts ready before the reading. The playwright can't expect the actor to prepare if the play is brought in the day of the reading, or worse yet, if a very rough draft is passed out to be read. (There is no more sickening feeling for the playwright or the participants in the cold reading than to have the reading progressing nicely only to come to a dead stop as an actor searches for a missing page, or if it turns out that the actors are reading different versions of the same script.)

Before the reading takes place the playwright should also take the responsibility for inviting whatever audience is wanted. If there are directors or dramaturges interested in you and your work, invite them to the cold reading. Be sure to seek them out for their response after the reading is over, so that they know you are interested in hearing their opinions. At the same time, a cold reading does not require an audience of two or three hundred people. That large an audience should be saved for the staged reading step in the process—or, better yet, for the full production. Too many people in the audience—especially if they are "strangers off the street"—are going to force the actors into performing. In a cold reading you don't want performances—you want good, intelligent readings. There is a difference, and a smaller, more friendly audience will help to ensure that you get readings of your roles rather than unrehearsed performances.

The reading itself should be scheduled so that the playwright has time to meet with the actors—even for just a few minutes—before the rest of the audience arrives. This allows time for questions to be asked, missing pages to be replaced, and introductions to be made. Regardless of whether the actors are being paid for their time, remember that their agreeing to be in your reading is a great favor to you and should be acknowledged as such.

To give some idea of how a cold reading actually takes place, we've selected the final scene from a play by Stephen Levi. Stephen attended Los Angeles City College before moving to New York to study acting with Stella Adler, Herbert Berghof, Uta Hagen, and Lee Strasberg. He has performed in regional theater and has written over twenty plays and eight screenplays. His first play, *Daphne in Cottage D,* was produced at Broadway's Longacre Theatre. *Cherry Soda Water, The Gulf of Crimson* and *Je T'aime, Jessica* were presented at HB Playwrights' Foundation, where he also taught playwriting. Two light comedies, *Angel on My Shoulder* and *Getting Mama Married,* are published by Samuel French. His *Goodbye, Victor,* with Michael Moriarty, was the premiere show for Chevrolet Theatre on USA-Cable TV. Stephen has had playwriting residencies at the Playwrights' Center in Minneapolis, the Pennsylvania Stage Company, SUNY/College at Brockport and, most recently, the Florida Studio Theatre in Sarasota.

The play of his that we've selected was titled, in this draft, *Memorial to the Honored Dead.* It underwent numerous rewrites as it passed through a process that included cold readings, a nonperformance workshop, staged readings, and a college workshop production.

In *Memorial to the Honored Dead,* fragments of time, place, and action are pieced together as a young man—through a series of visits to his mother who is in a mental institution—tries to untangle their love/hate relationship.

Imagine, if you will, that you are in a comfortable, well-lit theater space or workshop room. It does not have to be very large. Thirty to fifty seats is a good size, with an 8 foot by 12 foot "stage area." You've invited friends whose opinions you respect, and they are gathered around listening to your play. The stage manager is reading the stage direction that leads into the final scene, to give everyone a sense of what is happening in the scene. The scene originally read as follows:

Memorial to the Honored Dead: Original Script

(Lights up on sun room. SOUNDS of BIRDS CHIRPING OUTSIDE. MASIE is on the floor, a shoe box next to HER. SHE is striking matches, setting fire to imaginary photographs. HIS guitar beside HIM, the ORDERLY watches. JOHN approaches.)

JOHN

Hi.

MASIE

(Looks up, smiles sweetly.)

Oh, hi. Sit down.

JOHN

(Kneels.)

What're you doing?

MASIE

Burnin' pictures.

JOHN

Oh?

MASIE

Pictures from my box of pictures. This is the last one. See? It's my son an' me. Standin' in front of the Greyhound Bus Depot in Washington, D.C. After Jimmy's funeral we took the bus from Battletown to Washington, then a cab to the airport. Deke was fourteen at the time.

(SHE strikes a match. The photo burns.)

There. All done. He's gone. Dead. As if he never was.

(Turning to HIM; brightly.)

How are you today? It's been a while, hasn't it?

JOHN

(Preoccupied.)

Yes, it has.

MASIE

Been away makin' a movie?

JOHN

We went over schedule. So that's how you killed him?

MASIE

What?

JOHN

Your kid? That's how he died.

MASIE

Ashes to ashes. Dust to dust. I've killed him dozens of times. But this was the last. 'Cause in all these pictures there's no more of him. It's now jist a box of happy memories. Wanna look?

(SHE picks through the photos.)

Here's one of me when I was about fifteen. Look how long my hair was. An' my smile. I had a nice smile, didn't I?

JOHN

(Looks at HER.)

Yes, you did.

MASIE

(Laughs.)

I was always happy. Here I am at the beach. Will you look at that bathin' suit? I was a good swimmer. I could outswim all the boys.

JOHN

Yes, I know.

MASIE

An' look at me in my hula skirt. Boy, could I do the hula. Wiggle my hips. I don't think there was a dance invented that I couldn't do.

JOHN

(Smiles warmly.)

I'm sure.

MASIE

An' here I am at my easel. An' here's one of my paintin's. Calvin loved my paintin's. I think he was the only one of my husbands who really appreciated my artwork. Every time I'd finish a paintin' he'd bring out the Kodak. Lookit 'em all.

JOHN

There's a lot.

MASIE

Oh, my God! Here I am singin' at a party! Anytime there was a piano around I'd ask 'em to play, an' I'd git up an' sing. I didn't care who was there. I'd of sung for anyone, jist to be singin'.

(Frowns.)

Who's this with me?

(Shrugs.)

Beats me. You know, I never met a stranger. I could go right up an' talk to anyone. This picture proves it!

(Laughs.)

An' here . . . !

(SHE goes still.)

Oh, it's one I missed. It's Little Deke standin' outside the home place with his first birthday cake. That's me . . . an' Grandma Sisters . . . an' Jimmy Sisters . . . an' Little Deke.

(The ORDERLY picks up HIS guitar and starts to play "Shortnin' Bread.")

Such a happy little baby.

(SHE starts to cradle the imaginary child.)

Hello, Little Deke. Hello, my sweetie pie.

(SHE rises.)

You'll excuse us, won't you? I haven't been with my baby all day. He's been with Grandma Sisters. An' I wanna spend some time with him.

(Walking off.)

We've got a whole lifetime together. A whole lifetime.

(SHE sings.)

Mama's little baby loves
shortnin', shortnin',

Mama's little baby loves
shortnin' bread. . . .

(The ORDERLY follows HER as the lights fade on THEM.)

JOHN

(To the audience.)

Masie died shortly thereafter. I don't think she had the strength to go over it all again. When all things are said and done perhaps it's enough to love the past, or if not to love it, at least to accept it—the good and the bad, the pain and the comfort, the love and the hate. When they found Masie in her room, her arms were like this, and I knew . . . as an infant . . . I was in them.

CURTAIN

For the purposes of the cold reading you don't need most of the stage directions. Clues as to how the characters say their lines or react to other characters are usually not needed. Good actors, reading your script intelligently, will find stage directions valuable, but having them spoken out by the stage manager will be more of a distraction than a help. If anything, stage directions that don't read "true" and seem to need the help of a stage manager to convey (such as telling an actor to read a line in a "preoccupied" manner) might well be ones that the playwright should reconsider. Many playwrights will have a copy of the script in front of them as the cold reading progresses, and they'll make notes in the script of places they need to reconsider.

In doing a cold reading of *Memorial to the Honored Dead*, the director eliminated many of the stage directions from the original script to help make the reading go smoother. It is best to have the stage manager or the playwright physically strike out directions that are not to be read. This helps eliminate any questions the actors might have about which stage directions they should wait for before reading a line.

Here then is the same scene you just read, but marked for a cold reading.

Memorial to the Honored Dead: Cold Reading Script

(Lights up on sun room. SOUNDS of BIRDS CHIRPING OUTSIDE. MASIE is on the floor, a shoe box next to HER. SHE is striking matches, setting fire to imaginary photographs. HIS guitar beside HIM, the ORDERLY watches. JOHN approaches.)

JOHN

Hi.

MASIE

(~~Looks up, smiles sweetly~~)

Oh, hi. Sit down.

JOHN

(Kneels)

What're you doing?

MASIE

Burnin' pictures.

JOHN

Oh?

MASIE

Pictures from my box of pictures. This is the last one. See? It's my son an' me. Standin' in front of the Greyhound Bus Depot in Washington, D.C. After Jimmy's funeral we took the bus from Battletown to Washington, then a cab to the airport. Deke was fourteen at the time.

(SHE strikes a match. The photo burns.)

There. All done. He's gone. Dead. As if he never was.

(Turning to HIM; ~~brightly.~~)

How are you today? It's been a while, hasn't it?

JOHN

(~~Preoccupied.~~)

Yes, it has.

MASIE

Been away makin' a movie?

JOHN

We went over schedule. So that's how you killed him?

MASIE

What?

JOHN

Your kid? That's how he died.

MASIE

Ashes to ashes. Dust to dust. I've killed him dozens of times. But this was the last. 'Cause in all these pictures there's no more of him. It's now just a box of happy memories. Wanna look?

(SHE picks through the photos.)

Here's one of me when I was about fifteen. Look how long my hair was. An' my smile. I had an nice smile, didn't I?

JOHN

(~~Looks at HER.~~)

Yes, you did.

MASIE

(~~Laughs.~~)

I was always happy. Here I am at the beach. Will you look at that bathin' suit? I was a good swimmer. I could outswim all the boys.

JOHN

Yes, I know.

MASIE

An' look at me in my hula skirt. Boy, could I do the hula. Wiggle my hips. I don't think there was a dance invented that I couldn't do.

JOHN

(~~Smiles warmly.~~)

I'm sure.

MASIE

An' here I am at my easel. An' here's one of my paintin's. Calvin loved my paintin's. I think he was the only one of my husbands who really appreciated my artwork. Every time I'd finish a paintin' he'd bring out the Kodak. Lookit 'em all.

JOHN

There's a lot.

MASIE

Oh, my God! Here I am singin' at a party! Anytime there was a piano around I'd ask 'em to play, an' I'd git up an' sing. I didn't care who was there. I'd of sung for anyone, jist to be singin'.

(~~Frowns.~~)

Who's this with me?

(~~Shrugs.~~)

Beats me. You know, I never met a stranger. I could go right up an' talk to anyone. This picture proves it!

(~~Laughs.~~)

An' here . . . !

(~~SHE goes still.~~)

Oh, it's one I missed. It's Little Deke standin' outside the home place with his first birthday cake. That's me . . . an' Grandma Sisters . . . an' Jimmy Sisters . . . an' Little Deke.

(The ORDERLY picks up HIS guitar and starts to play "Shortnin' Bread.")

Such a happy little baby.

(SHE starts to cradle the imaginary child.)

Hello, Little Deke. Hello, my sweetie pie.

(SHE rises.)

You'll excuse us, won't you? I haven't been with my baby all day. He's been with Grandma Sisters. An' I wanna spend some time with him.

(Walking off.)

We've got a whole lifetime together. A whole lifetime.

(~~SHE sings.~~)

Mama's little baby loves
shortnin', shortnin',
Mama's little baby loves
shortnin' bread . . .

(The ORDERLY follows HER as the lights fade on them.)

JOHN

(To the audience.)

Masie died shortly thereafter. I don't think she had the strength to go over it all again. When all things are said and done perhaps it's enough to love the past, or if not to love it, at least to accept it—the good and the bad, the pain and the comfort, the love and the hate. When they found Masie in her room, her arms were like this, and I knew . . . as an infant . . . I was in them.

CURTAIN

Cold readings are one of the most helpful aspects of the play development process. They are the least expensive in terms of both time and dollars. They also provide one of the most fundamental services a playwright needs—they allow the playwright to hear the play with a fresh ear. If done well, a cold reading can also give a playwright a sense of where the play is going and what rewrites should be considered.

Encouraging audience feedback is an important aspect of

the cold reading. Many workshops build in an audience discussion as part of their process. These discussions can be run by the resident dramaturge or artistic director. Such discussions have mixed results. If they are conducted by an experienced artistic person, they can generate questions and comments that are helpful, sometimes illuminating. It is important to make sure that the discussions don't encourage having everyone in the audience tell the playwright how to write his or her play.

Another method of getting feedback is to have the playwright approach people on an individual basis either immediately after the reading in an informal reception setting, or by phone or by individual meetings after the reading. Again, we should stress that if you personally invite someone to your reading, you owe that person the courtesy of eliciting his or her comments afterward.

A good method of ensuring feedback on a cold reading is to organize a panel who will discuss your work after the reading. If you use a panel, then let those who will be on the panel know that you want them to stay for a discussion of the script after the cold reading. Give each of them a copy of your script to refer to certain pages when they want to discuss something specific.

The panel should have a moderator. Ideally, the person moderating should be familiar with the script, but should be neither the playwright nor the director. If you are having the play read through a theater or a workshop, the person in charge of that theater or workshop should be the moderator. But if the reading is done at your own home, then select a moderator who is intelligent, good at eliciting conversation, and professional enough to encourage some criticism of your play as well as some praise.

An important part of the panel's discussion is what should happen next with the script. More and more workshops have a developmental process that moves from the cold reading stage into a nonperformance workshop stage. The panel can be useful in helping both the writer and the staff of the workshop in determining if the script is ready to be "work-shopped."

The Nonperformance Workshop

After you have heard your play given a cold reading, you will probably notice certain parts of the script that aren't working. You'll want to rework those problem spots before trying to get your play staged or given a staged reading. At this point the best strategy is not to go running to your typewriter, but rather to get together with a group of actors and a director who are willing to "workshop" your play.

Some theatrical companies offer writers nonperformance workshops. For a period of a week or two, actors and a director will get together with you to act out your play and to find solutions for parts of the script that aren't working. No performance comes out of this work; rather, the work is done to help prepare the playwright for rewrites he or she wants to make.

Write to your local theater companies and see if they are interested in workshopping your script. Also contact college theater departments. Perhaps you can find a helpful professor who would like to have his or her directing or acting class work on your script.

But if you can't find a group to workshop your script, consider putting together your own nonperformance workshop. All it requires is a good group of actors, a shrewd director, a large room to work in, and you.

No play will ever be hurt by workshop work that is not geared toward performance, and most will be helped by it. John Olive, one of the most accomplished of the regional playwrights in the country, has done nonperformance workshop work on most of his plays at either the Playwrights' Center in Minneapolis or at the Wisdom Bridge Theater in Chicago. He has been quoted as saying, "It is hard to imagine bringing a play into a production rehearsal without its having had at least one nonperformance workshop."

We agree with John and many other playwrights who have been excited by this new technique. You should start thinking about the nonperformance workshop for your play even as you are organizing the first cold reading. Actors and directors enjoy being part of this process. It gives them a chance to have creative input into development of the play without the pressure of getting a play ready for opening night. No critic will destroy an actor's or a director's work if the work is done in a nonperformance setting. A playwright does not have to destroy a script if it "fails" in a nonperformance workshop. If a workshop is truly nonperformance, it cannot be a failure.

The keys to a successful nonperformance workshop are: (1) The focus has to be away from performance. If time is spent dealing only with acting or directing problems, then the focus will not be on the script. (2) The nonperformance workshop should be flexible. An intelligent director who works more as a "conductor" than a director can make all the difference in creating a flexible atmosphere for the workshop.

The flexibility of a nonperformance workshop has to be defined. That's why it is helpful if the director who assisted you with the cold reading can also be involved with the workshop. If there have been discussions between the playwright and the director before the nonperformance workshop begins about the goals of the workshop, and if a dramaturge—someone whose job it is to comment on scripts—has been invited to work with the playwright and the director in these discussions, then the chances for a successful workshop are much greater. The easiest way to define the parameters of the nonperformance workshop is to strike a bargain between director and playwright.

For example, everyone agrees that the first act of the play is working well. The playwright is expressing him or herself in a clear and meaningful way in the first act, and the audiences that have heard the script are engaged by the material. Perhaps the goal of the nonperformance workshop might be to explore problems in the second act. Maybe the play is actually a long one act. Dramatically no act break may make better sense—especially when plays such as *Passion*, *Talley's Folly,* and *'Night, Mother* have changed our ideas of what a full evening of theater is.

A director might suggest that the first workshop session should be spent reading through the play—around a table, with no movement—straight through, possibly looking for cuts and rearranging dramatic moments to make the script a long one act. It is important in a nonperformance workshop that the actors don't prepare but instead approach the material fresh. It is equally important that time be built into the workshop for all the participants to get a chance to express their thoughts concerning the work. For instance, after reading through the play without a break, the director might ask the actors to talk about whether they think the play works as a long one act or not. A director might also ask the actors to suggest scenes or parts of scenes that could be cut if cutting is one of the goals this session. (One of the advantages of the nonperformance process is that nothing has to be set—cuts can be put back in, the play can go back to being two acts, etc.)

A common problem for writers is what David Mamet calls "their inability to tell a story." (He is also the first to admit that one of his major problems as a young playwright was this inability to engage audiences in a credible story. His 1984 Pulitzer Prize–winning play, *Glengarry Glen Ross*, is proof that he solved his problem very well.) If a play has very solid characters, if there is a strong sense of mood and texture in the piece, if the theme seems well integrated into the style of the writing, then a nonperformance workshop might be aimed at exploring the story of the play. Good actors usually have rehearsal experience with improvisation, and a director working as a conductor can set up situations that might help to show the playwright possibilities for further development and work. Again, a strength of the nonperformance workshop process is that the structure is flexible enough to include several days of improvisational work if all agree that this work is getting to the core of the problems in the script.

One problem common to many new playwrights is that their plays often lack depth. There is no subtext to the scripts. The plays tend to be two-dimensional and ultimately less interesting than a play that both tells and suggests in the same dramatic action or beat. The nonperformance workshop is a perfect forum for exploring subtext and the nuances that good subtext creates.

At the same time the nonperformance workshop can be used to cut through subtext that is too dense, or too convoluted. Many playwrights get carried away with the possibilities of live theater, and weave a text that is all subtext to the point that all surface story and dramatic tension is lost. A solution to these problems can be found by having a straightforward discussion of motivations of the characters versus author's intent.

Any nonperformance workshop depends on healthy give and take between the participants. A playwright must approach a workshop with an open and receptive attitude, and the actors, the director, and the dramaturge have to come into the workshop ready to ask questions and be part of a positive dialogue about the play.

Most playwrights find it very helpful to be able to spread the nonperformance workshop out over a period of time that is long enough to permit rewriting. One process that is being used increasingly when time permits is for the workshop participants to gather together for a day or two each week over a three- to five-week period (e.g., every Monday and Wednesday for three weeks, or every Saturday for five weeks). This style of nonperformance workshop allows the maximum amount of flexibility and at the same time enables a playwright who is ready to work to do an amazing amount of rewriting in this relatively short period of time.

Now for a look at the Stephen Levi script. Note the deletions that have been made in the material as well as the notes made on problem areas in the script.

Memorial to the Honored Dead: Nonperformance Workshop Script and Comments

(Lights up on sun room. SOUNDS OF BIRDS CHIRPING OUTSIDE. MASIE is on the floor, a shoe box next to HER. SHE
(A) is striking matches, setting fire to imaginary

In a nonperformance workshop the physical actions of the play can be explored in much greater depth than can be usually done in either a cold reading or a staged reading.

photographs. HIS guitar beside HIM, the ORDERLY watches. JOHN approaches.)

JOHN

Hi.

MASIE

(~~Looks up, smiles sweetly~~)

Oh, hi. Sit down.

JOHN

(Kneels.)

What're you doing?

MASIE

Burnin' pictures.

JOHN

Oh?

MASIE

Pictures from my box of pictures. This is the last one. See? It's my son an' me. Standin' in front of the Greyhound Bus Depot in Washington, D.C. After Jimmy's funeral we took the bus from Battletown to Washington, then a cab to the airport. Deke was fourteen at the time.

Ⓑ (SHE strikes a match. The photo burns.)

There. All done. He's gone. Dead. As if he never was.

A question that might be posed by the director/conductor to the actress reading Masie concerning the stage direction marked by letter Ⓐ is "What does this action mean in terms of the story that we already know and in terms of the rest of the play?" Does the action "striking matches" seem specific enough, does it ring true, will it be comfortable, etc.

This discussion can continue through to the very specific action indicated in Ⓑ. "SHE strikes a match. The photo burns." Is this action becoming something more, or is it subtext? And if it is subtext, where is it leading us? Especially in light of Ⓒ, where her mood seems to be shifting even faster than we've seen it shifting

Ⓒ (<u>Turning to HIM; brightly.</u>)

How are you today? It's been quite a while, hasn't it?

JOHN

Ⓓ (<u>Preoccupied.</u>)
Yes, it has.

MASIE

Been away makin' a movie?

JOHN

We went over schedule. So that's how you killed him?

MASIE

What?

JOHN

Your kid? That's how he died.

MASIE

Ashes to ashes. Dust to dust. I've killed him dozens of times. But this was the last. 'Cause in all these pictures there's no more of him. It's now jist a box of happy memories. Wanna look?

(SHE picks through the photos.)

Here's one of me when I was about fifteen. Look how long my hair was. An' my smile. I had a nice smile, didn't I?

before. Is the build in tempo leading to a heightened dramatic effect?

And then what is happening with the character of the son John? In Ⓓ the playwright has him being "preoccupied." What is causing this preoccupation; how will an audience interpret this? Is the dramatic action of the photo burning going to take all of the focus here? What might an actor suggest for ways he can take focus back? Does the playwright want this?

JOHN
(~~Looks at HER.~~)
Yes, you did.

MASIE
(~~Laughs.~~)
Ⓔ I was always happy. Here I am at the beach. Will you look at that bathin' suit? I was a good swimmer. I could outswim all the boys.

JOHN
Yes, I know.

MASIE
An' look at me in my hula skirt. Boy, could I do the hula. Wiggle my hips. I don't think there was a dance invented that I couldn't do.

JOHN
(~~Smiles warmly.~~)
I'm sure.

MASIE
An' here I am at my easel. An' here's one of my paintin's. Calvin loved my paintin's. I think he was the only one of my husbands who really appreciated my artwork. Every time I'd finish a paintin' he'd bring out the Kodak. Lookit 'em all.

JOHN
There's a lot.

In Ⓔ Masie is slipping back into a memory, but this memory is an active memory. It is triggered by something concrete—a photo that she is burning.

MASIE

Oh, my God! Here I am singin' at a party! Anytime there was a piano around I'd ask 'em to play, an' I'd git up an' sing. I didn't care who was there. I'd of sung for anyone, jist to be singin'.

(~~Frowns.~~)

Ⓕ Who's this with me?

(~~Shrugs.~~)

Beats me. You know, I never met a stranger. I could go right up an' talk to anyone. This picture proves it!

(~~Laughs.~~)

An' here . . . !

Ⓖ (~~SHE goes still.~~)

Oh, it's one I missed. It's Little Deke standin' outside the home place with his first birthday cake. That's me . . . an' Grandma Sisters . . . an' Jimmy Sisters . . . an' Little Deke.

Ⓗ (The ORDERLY picks up HIS guitar and starts to play SHORTNIN' BREAD.)

Such a happy little baby.

In Ⓕ she actually engages her son in the photograph/ memory by asking him "Who's this with me?" Can we believe after this action that he is still preoccupied? What is it the playwright wants from us concerning our responses to John and Masie at this point near the end of the play? Throughout the play there has been a "third character." He is at once an orderly and many other smaller cameo roles. As Masie seems to pause for just a moment in her active rememberings Ⓖ all of a sudden the orderly comes back into the play.

Is this jarring in Ⓗ? Does it take away from the dramatic build or add to it? Why "SHORTNIN' BREAD"?

(I) (SHE starts to cradle the imaginary child.)

Hello, Little Deke. Hello my sweetie pie.

(~~SHE rises.~~)

You'll excuse us, won't you? I haven't been with my baby all day. He's been with Grandma Sisters. An' I wanna spend some time with him.

(Walking off.)

We've got a whole lifetime together. A whole lifetime.

(SHE sings.)

MAMA'S LITTLE BABY LOVES SHORTNIN'
SHORTNIN', MAMA'S LITTLE BABY LOVES
SHORTNIN' BREAD . . .

(J) (~~The ORDERLY follows HER as the lights fade on THEM.~~)

JOHN
(To the audience.)
Masie died shortly thereafter. I don't think she had the strength to go over it all again. When all things

Has that song been set up enough or too much for us earlier in the play?

In (I) Masie seems by her actions to be totally lost in memory. Is this going to be too strong an image (that of her cradling the imaginary child)?

What do we read into the final action of the orderly following her as John does the final speech? What mood are we left with by this ending, following (J)?

are said and done perhaps
it's enough to love the past,
or if not to love it, at least
to accept it—the good and
the bad, the pain and the
comfort, the love and the
hate. When they found
Masie in her room, her
arms were like this, and I
knew . . . as an infant . . . I
was in them.

CURTAIN

A nonperformance workshop is not automatically going to guarantee a better play, but it does help to solve problem areas of the script. Some playwrights use a nonperformance workshop to polish a script, whereas others use it as a way of taking a play apart and truly testing the spine or structure of the play itself. Somewhere in between these two extremes you'll find a way of working on your script that is right. That is the beauty of the nonperformance workshop as a developmental technique.

The Staged Reading

Unlike the cold reading, the staged reading makes use of movement. Actors usually stand up, scripts in hand, and act out your play. A staged reading is one that usually requires a minimum of 12 to 15 hours of rehearsal and a maximum of about 40. Much less than this and the reading is not really staged (although an interesting exercise for actors is to "improvise" the actions of a script with absolutely no direction) and much more than 40 hours of rehearsal and you might as well do a production. In simplest terms, to stage a reading means to put it on its feet. The important movement that has to be read in a cold reading or even a nonperformance workshop is acted out. Depending upon how elaborate the staging is, even things like sound effects and background music can be worked into a staged reading. Usually the stage is set by the director or the stage manager before the reading actually begins, and if there are numerous time and place changes that might be confusing, a word or two can be said during the transitions, but normally no directions are given once the reading starts. Instead, the actors do their best—holding the scripts —to act out the movement of the play.

Thus Stephen Levi's script might well look like the following for a staged reading. It is quite possible that the three directions left in (the beginning direction, the last direction, and "curtain") would also be omitted if the theater would spend a couple of hours doing technical business such as recording sound and working out a fade-out at the end. Here is a staged reading script of the last scene of *Memorial to the Honored Dead*. It is missing everything but the actors' directions or blocking marks.

Memorial to the Honored Dead: Staged Reading Script

Lights up on sun room. SOUNDS OF BIRDS CHIRPING OUTSIDE. ~~MASIE is on the floor, a shoe box next to HER. SHE is striking matches, setting fire to imaginary photographs. HIS guitar beside HIM, the ORDERLY watches JOHN approaches.~~)

JOHN

Hi.

MASIE

(~~Looks up, smiles sweetly.~~)

Oh, hi. Sit down.

JOHN

(~~Kneels.~~)

What're you doing?

MASIE

Burnin' pictures.

JOHN

Oh?

MASIE

Pictures from my box of pictures. This is the last one. See? It's my son an' me. Standin' in front of the Greyhound Bus Depot in Washington, D.C. After Jimmy's funeral we took the bus from Battletown to Washington, then a cab to the airport. Deke was fourteen at the time.

(~~SHE strikes a match. The photo burns.~~)

There. All done. He's gone. Dead. As if he never was.

(~~Turning to HIM, brightly.~~)

How are you today? It's been a while, hasn't it?

JOHN

(~~Preoccupied.~~)

Yes, it has.

MASIE

Been away makin' a movie?

JOHN

We went over schedule. So that's how you killed him?

MASIE

What?

JOHN

Your kid? That's how he died.

MASIE

Ashes to ashes. Dust to dust. I've killed him dozens of times. But this was the last. 'Cause in all these pictures there's no more of him. It's now jist a box of happy memories. Wanna look?

(~~SHE picks through the photos.~~)

Here's one of me when I was about fifteen. Look how long my hair was. An' my smile. I had a nice smile, didn't I?

JOHN

(~~Looks at HER.~~)

Yes, you did.

MASIE

(~~Laughs.~~)

I was always happy. Here I am at the beach. Will you look at that bathin' suit? I was a good swimmer. I could outswim all the boys.

JOHN

Yes, I know.

MASIE

An' look at me in my hula skirt. Boy, could I do the hula. Wiggle my hips. I don't think there was a dance invented that I couldn't do.

JOHN

(~~Smiles warmly.~~)

I'm sure.

MASIE

An' here I am at my easel. An' here's one of my paintin's. Calvin loved my paintin's. I think he was the only one of my husbands who really appreciated my artwork. Every time I'd finish a paintin' he'd bring out the Kodak. Lookit 'em all.

JOHN

There's a lot.

MASIE

Oh, my God! Here I am singin' at a party! Anytime there was a piano around I'd ask 'em to play, an' I'd git up an' sing. I didn't care who was there. I'd of sung for anyone, jist to be singin'.

(~~Frowns.~~)

Who's this with me?

(~~Shrugs.~~)

Beats me. You know, I never met a stranger. I could go right up an' talk to anyone. This picture proves it!

(~~Laughs.~~)

An' here . . . !

(~~SHE goes still.~~)

Oh, it's one I missed. It's Little Deke standin' outside the home place with his first birthday cake. That's me . . . an' Grandma Sisters . . . an' Jimmy Sisters . . . an' Little Deke.

(~~The ORDERLY picks up HIS guitar and starts to play SHORTNIN' BREAD.~~)

Such a happy little baby.

(~~SHE starts to cradle the imaginary child.~~)

Hello, Little Deke. Hello, my sweetie pie.

(~~SHE rises.~~)

You'll excuse us, won't you? I haven't been with my baby all day. He's been with Grandma Sisters. An' I wanna spend some time with him.

(~~Walking off.~~)

We've got a whole lifetime together. A whole lifetime.

(~~She sings.~~)

MAMA'S LITTLE BABY LOVES
SHORTNIN', SHORTNIN',
MAMA'S LITTLE BABY LOVES
SHORTNIN' BREAD . . .

(~~The ORDERLY follows HER as the lights fade on THEM.~~)

JOHN

(~~To the audience.~~)

Masie died shortly thereafter. I don't think she had the strength to go over it all again. When all things are said and done perhaps it's enough to love the past, or if not to love it, at least to accept it—the good and the bad, the pain and the comfort, the love and the hate. When they found Masie in her room, her arms were like this, and I knew . . . as an infant . . . I was in them.

CURTAIN

If you have been sending your script around faithfully and if the play has been improving as you go through the developmental steps, then chances are good, you'll be offered a staged reading by one of the companies who has read your play.

But even if no one is interested in giving you a staged reading, there are ways to get it set up. If actors from your nonperformance workshop are still available and interested, you can work out a schedule with them.

Many actors dislike staged readings because they require as much or more concentration and work as a full production, but with none of the luxury of the rehearsal time to get to know the characters, the play, and each other. The irony here is that good actors are a must for a successful staged reading. If the playwright is going to learn anything at all from seeing a play on its feet and from hearing an audience's responses to the play on its feet, then he or she has to have the best possible actors in each role. An experienced actor is going to have a hard time making a kiss work while both he and his partner are holding scripts. (Kisses and fights are two of the most difficult staged reading techniques, even for veteran actors—what usually happens is dialogue is stopped or memorized in short bursts to cover the movement so that the movement can be seen unencumbered by the scripts in hand.)

Casting becomes very important to the successful reading. Rather than posting sign-up sheets for actors or recruiting loyal friends who might not be right for a particular role, in the staged reading you need to seek experience and type in your actors. If a script calls for a very tall woman to fall in love with a very short man, then for the staged reading you should be able to cast a very tall actress and a very short actor; otherwise the reading is not going to work in the same way that a cold reading of the script might work. Casting for a staged reading should be done as much like casting for a full production as possible. Looking through résumés and selecting actors that seem to be the right physical type, and then doing callbacks that include readings from the script is the best way to cast a staged reading. If this seems like a lot of work for the 20 or so hours of actual rehearsal time and reading, then perhaps you can understand why we feel that less emphasis on staged readings and a bit more emphasis on nonperformance workshops are important for theaters that truly are "for the playwright" in terms of developmental work.

Selection of a director is equally as important as casting. The wrong director can impede the reading by not getting into the meaning of the script fast enough, thus wasting valuable staging time. A director must be quick in order to do staged readings. He or she has to have an intuitive sense that will be used to make choices which are instinctually right. Analytical time in a staged reading rehearsal process is necessarily nonexistent. Directors who over-intellectualize a play or who want to check every movement choice with the playwright will have a hard time making a staged reading look good. Certain directors who are very good at staging readings are developing in this country. Soon there will be courses to teach this technique in universities. For many young directors in a city such as New York, the first few showcases they are given access to with professional actors are actually staged readings of new plays. For the sake of the playwright, let's hope that these directors are working on material that is ready to be showcased as well. Otherwise, the response of the audience might well be "Great acting, exciting new director, but too bad about the choice of play." To help avoid this type of response to a staged reading, it is important to set up the format of the evening just right.

By setting up the format, we don't just mean making sure the lights are on and the seats are set up. We mean that the publicity for the staged reading (if there has to be publicity) clearly indicates that this is a work-in-progress and not a showcase. If programs will be distributed at the reading, the program should also stress the developmental nature of the evening. Most important, a disclaimer should be addressed to the audience by the artistic director of the theater or the workshop. This disclaimer is to protect the playwright by emphasizing that what the audience is about to see is a work-in-progress, not a finished play.

Another important factor in the staged reading format is the use of the audience. If you have invited an audience to be part of your developmental process by watching the staged reading, then it is courteous to give them a chance to respond more actively to the work than by laughing, crying, or applauding. A well-run after-the-reading discussion can be beneficial if the playwright is ready for this informal critique. A technique that Dale Wasserman (author of the musical book for *Man of La Mancha* and the stage adaptation of *One Flew Over the Cuckoo's Nest*) used for years at the Midwest Playwrights Conference while he served as the Artistic Director was to give out a questionnaire with the programs for each audience member to fill out after the reading, or else to take home with them and send back in. An amazingly high percentage of these critique forms came back in—either handed to ushers after the reading or mailed back within a few days after the reading. The questions from these questionnaires may suggest what types of responses are generally helpful, whether they be written or verbal.

SAMPLE AUDIENCE QUESTIONNAIRE

In order to provide the playwright with feedback on tonight's play, we need your comments. We are particularly interesting in the following:

WHAT DID YOU LIKE?

WHEN WERE YOU CONFUSED?

WAS THERE ANYTHING YOU DIDN'T LIKE?

WHAT DID YOU ACTIVELY DISLIKE?

WERE YOU BORED? (IF SO, WHEN?)

OTHER COMMENTS:

There are as many ways to do a staged reading as there are directors to interpret a script and then put it on its feet. All of the following are variations of ways to hold your reading. Each was successful in its own way, and might be worth considering for a specific staged reading or a series of staged readings.

—Using a set specifically built for staged readings. The O'Neill National Playwrights Conference has a lovely set of interchangeable cubes and metal forms that can be made into a great variety of shapes by adding a piece of plywood held on by C-clamps.
—The Artistic Director of the Professional Theatre at Cornell University, David Feldshuh, has his actors—in character—tell us when they are doing a large physical ac-

tion. This technique keeps the actors from having to deal with props and at the same time makes for a more intense experience than simply using an imaginary prop. A reading of a Paul D'Andrea script titled *Bully* David staged in New York illustrates this interesting directorial style:

CLAY

(the actor says this): "Raises his rifle and looks her right in the eye—without moving for the longest time—he then speaks."

What did you say?

—The Arena Stage in Washington, D.C., came up with some innovations in the mid-1970s to help make their reading series more interesting to audience members, while at the same time stressing the developmental nature of the process. They used well-known actors and actresses in their staged reading series, and then asked the audience to return on subsequent evenings to see what changes the playwright had made in the script. Discussion was based on the merits of those changes (or lack of same). It was a short-lived but popular staged reading series.
—The Playwrights Platform of Boston, in an idea modified from the O'Neill National Playwrights Conference, hires local set designers to do a rendering of a possible setting for the play. This rendering is placed on an easel in the lobby of the theater before the reading, and is incorporated into the audience discussion after the reading to help give clarity to the visual aspect of a play that is almost totally lost in a staged reading—the design of the piece.
—The most successful staged readings generally use a minimum of props or even suggested costumes. The general rule for staged readings is that if a prop is necessary to help get the meaning of a moment across to an audience, then the writer probably needs to do more work.

—On a colorful note, several workshops have their playwrights do rewrites on different colored paper. Thus a second draft will be yellow, a third draft blue, and so on.

—And in a move back toward the style of chamber readings in the 1930s, we've seen staged readings in which the actors stand at music stands, and for emphasis let the pages fall to the ground as they finish them. If this sounds reminiscent of the radio dramas of the Golden Age of Radio, then you realize where the first idea for a staged reading might well have come from—radio.

So what is the advantage of holding a staged reading? What makes them worthwhile despite the fact that they take careful casting, frenetic rehearsal time, and luck in finding a director? The staged reading does serve as an important last step in a developmental process. It allows a playwright to see things that he or she might not see in a cold reading or a nonperformance workshop. A staged reading also gives an audience more for its "admission dollar" than a cold reading. But staged readings were never intended to be the final step for a play in terms of its full life. Productions should be the ultimate goal of any playwright, and a script that is not being reworked and developed toward the goal of a production is the script that is a waste of everyone's time.

If the trend toward doing staged readings rather than productions continues, then perhaps it will be necessary for granting agencies and unions, such as the Actors' Equity Association or the Dramatists Guild, to step in and assert the need for staged readings to be part of a process that leads to productions rather than the end of a play's life. With this editorial comment in mind, let's lay out some ideas concerning organizing your own staged reading.

The key to a successful staged reading is knowing when the play is ready to be staged as a reading. If you have had one or more cold readings of the play and it seems to sound right to you; if you have had the opportunity to explore the language of the script in nonperformance workshop sessions and you don't feel you can learn anything more about the play until you see it on its feet, then it is probably ready for a staged reading.

Find yourself a place that is conducive to the reading. It does not necessarily have to be a stage. Indeed, sometimes staged readings done on a stage are self-defeating. The audience comes expecting something much closer to a production, and is quickly disappointed, which tends to color its response to what it is seeing. One of the most natural spaces in this country for staged readings is the O'Neill National Playwright Conference's outdoor theater. Located right under a giant beech tree from which the play *Summertree* takes its name, this location provides the proper combination of a nontheatrical space that allows viewers to focus on the play and not on the trappings of the physical plant. Another good space for staged readings is the Lindsay/Crouse Studio (named after Howard Lindsay and Russel Crouse—two of the founders) in the New Dramatists' building on Forty-fourth Street in midtown Manhattan. This space features seating units that roll, unfocused overhead strip lighting, and a stage that is less than 10 by 12 feet.

Once you have determined where and when, then start your work to draw an audience. The best places for staged readings are usually small, so forty to sixty people can make a good audience for a staged reading. Expanding on the list of friends and professional acquaintances who you would invite to a cold reading, go ahead and send a simple flyer—stressing that the play is a work-in-progress. (Let the audience tell you afterward that the play is ready for production—don't you tell them before the reading.)

As if borrowing the worst aspects of the nonprofit developmental theater world, many commercial producers are now offering staged readings of plays as backers' auditions. Rather than presenting forty-five well-chosen and well-staged minutes of a play that they are interested in getting investors for, some commercial producers are actually dressing up the actors in their Sunday-best and doing a staged reading of the entire script. Under no circumstances should this technique of staging a reading become the final step that means the life or the death of the play. A visual artist/designer attended a staged reading of Tom's a few years ago, and expressed dismay months later when he learned that the theater had decided not to produce the play because the staged reading hadn't quite worked. To him this was akin to looking at a black-and-white photograph of one of his paintings and then deciding, based on that glimpse at the photograph, whether or not the painting should be purchased.

Enough said.

The Easiest Way to Get Your Play Noticed

Getting to know people . . . Getting people to read your scripts . . . Getting a cold reading organized . . . Trying to get people to your cold reading so they can help you put together a nonperformance workshop . . . Doing a nonperformance workshop to try and polish and improve the play . . . Trying to get someone interested enough in your play to do a staged reading of the play so you can see what you have. All this might seem like a long, involved process, and it is. Many writers can spend three to five to fifty years working on and developing their scripts. Fifty years? Cases in point—the past three Pultizer Prize–winning playwrights: Tony Kushner, Edward Albee and Horton Foote. Tony is one of the youngest Pulitzer winners. His *Angels in America* was a commission from the Eureka Theatre in San Francisco. A series of readings in a number of workshops around the country led to a production in London. The work was considered too big and too long for American theaters in this era of cutbacks and caution, but once the play did well in London it found producers in Los Angeles and then on Broadway. Now, some ten years later, *Angels* is touring and getting numerous regional productions. Edward Albee is an Off-Broadway icon who, like Tennessee Williams and so many other great American playwrights, had trouble getting productions in mid career. *Three Tall Women* was also first produced in Europe in the mid-1980s and then largely ignored until the McCarter Theatre, under playwright Emily Mann's control, produced the play in 1993. It came to New York City as part of a season of Albee works produced by the Signature Theatre (one of America's most important companies for living playwrights) and won Edward his second Pulitzer in 1994. Horton Foote has been working on a series of plays about small town Texan life ever since he was a New Dramatists member in the late 1940s. Almost fifty years later one of these works, *The Young Man from Atlanta,* also produced at the Signature Theatre, won him the 1995 Pulitzer.

Does every playwright go through this long, involved developmental process? Was Chekhov suggesting some sort of cruel, ironic joke when he said that a writer for the theater should not spend more than a month on the first draft of his play? (And then nine years on the next draft?) With each playwright, with each play, the germination time of the play as it goes from idea to paper to reading to rewrite to production is different. But more and more successful playwrights are getting involved in formal playwrights' workshops, which can eliminate much of the tedious detail work of setting up a cold reading, getting people interested in the play, working on putting together a nonperformance workshop, and so on.

All of these functioning workshops are constantly looking for new writers. Each has different methods of working depending on their charters, their budgets, their locations, but a playwright can be helped immensely by having access to one or more of these programs.

On the following pages are listings of the ten most successful ongoing workshops for playwrights. Be aware that there are always new workshops starting up—indeed a recent trend has been for producing theaters to start their own playwrights' workshops. These listings should not be considered all-inclusive. We also would encourage you to think about starting your own workshop if there is nothing in your geographic area.

Playwrights' Workshops

Alliance Theatre Company's New Voices

The last decade has seen many changes in Atlanta's theater community. Seven theaters that once did annual festivals of new works are now either out of business or not aggressively producing new works. Instead, Atlanta's largest and most venerable theatre—the Alliance—is taking a leadership role in new play development. Three plays a year are chosen for workshop work, with some going on to full production.

WHO: Playwrights of color.

STAFF: Walter Bilderback, Dramaturg

APPLICATION: Unproduced play and application form.

ADDRESS: Alliance Theatre, 1280 Peachtree Street, NE, Atlanta, GA 30309. (404) 898-1132

Bay Area Playwrights Festival

Takes place annually during the months of July and August. The festival brings together members of the collaborative process. Each summer selected playwrights, librettists, composers, choreographers, directors, actors, and others are invited to join together in the exploration of and creation of experimental works. The Bay Area Playwrights Festival has been the environment for collaborators of an improvisational opera, plays with music, video/theater work, and so on.

WHO: Playwrights, composers, librettists, etc.

STAFF: Mame Hunt, Artistic Director

APPLICATION: Submit works or properties. Each workshop varies as to thematic and stylistic approaches. So definitely contact them before applying.

ADDRESS: Box 460357, San Francisco, CA 94114. (415) 255-2254

Denver Center Theatre Company US West Workshop

One of the interesting changes in the last few years of new play development is that more and more workshops are being hosted by large theater companies. This gives a workshop stability and access to gifted professional artists who are "on staff." This workshop is a perfect example of that trend.

WHO: Playwrights who have written an unproduced full-length play with more than one character.

STAFF: Tom Szentgyorgyi, Associate Artistic Director

APPLICATION: Write for guidelines.

ADDRESS: 1050 13th Street, Denver, CO 80204.

First Stage

This is one of our favorite of the many new workshops for playwrights in the country. First Stage offers weekly staged readings of both plays and screenplays (this is L.A., after all); access to very talented member actors, directors, and dramaturgs; and regular playwriting and screenwriting workshops. Also, for a $25 contribution, this company will guarantee a professional staged reading of a ten-minute play of yours as part of their annual fund-raising marathon.

WHO: Any playwright or screenwriter.

STAFF: Dennis Safren, Literary Manager

APPLICATION: Submit script for reading slot. Membership fee of $50 pays for interesting newsletter subscription and workshops.

ADDRESS: 6817 Franklin Avenue, Los Angeles, CA 90028.

New Dramatists

This is the country's oldest service organization for playwrights. Founded in 1949 by Michaela O'Harra, Howard Lindsay, Moss Hart, and their colleagues, New Dramatists provides the time, space, and tools for playwrights to develop their craft. Programs include: readings of works-in-progress, a new play library, loan fund, and rooms for short-term residencies while in New York City.

WHO: Open to New York City residents and national members who can spend a reasonable length of time each season in New York.

STAFF: Paul Slee, Managing Director

APPLICATION: Submit two full-length scripts, résumé, and (if applying for national membership) a letter of recommendation from a theater professional.

ADDRESS: 424 West 44th Street, New York, NY 10036.

O'Neill National Playwright's Conference

This country's largest nonproducing workshop. The O'Neill Theater Center began in 1964 and spawned a number of projects over the next few years. One of these was the National Playwright's Conference—a place for playwrights to work with other theater professionals on the development of their new scripts. The conference is held each summer, with playwrights in residence for one month on the grounds of the former Eugene O'Neill estate in Waterford, Connecticut.

WHO: Playwrights and screenwriters.

STAFF: George C. White, President
Lloyd Richards, Artistic Director

APPLICATION: Write to O'Neill Theater Center for application form. (Deadline is December 1, and note: this is the only workshop that charges a fee to apply.)

ADDRESS: 234 West 44th Street, New York, NY 10036.

The Playwrights' Center of Minnesota

The authors of this book first met and worked together here. The organization was founded in 1971 by playwrights Erik Brogger, Gar Hildenbrand, Barbara Field, and Gregg Almquist. The Playwrights' Center serves playwrights year round through several ongoing programs: the Playwrights' Lab, the Midwest Playlabs, the McKnight Fellowships, Jerome grants, Jones One Act Commissions, and Shop Talks.

WHO: Open to playwright members (there are several categories of membership).

STAFF: Lisa Stevens, Membership Director

APPLICATION: Write for more information, as each category of membership has separate procedures and deadlines.

ADDRESS: 2301 Franklin Avenue E, Minneapolis, MN 55406.

Playwrights Forum

A ten-year-old organization based in Washington, D.C., and serving playwrights throughout the mid-Atlantic region. Its aim is to provide playwrights with the opportunity to meet with their peers for the purpose of improving their professional competence and marketing skills. Various units meet regularly for readings of works-in-progress and discussions with theater professionals.

WHO: Playwrights who live in the mid-Atlantic region. All members must pay an annual fee.

STAFF: Ernest Joselovitz, Administrator

APPLICATION: Write for details, as each unit of the forum has different procedures and deadlines.

ADDRESS: Box 11488, Washington, DC 20008-0688.

Shenandoah International Playwrights Retreat

A true rural retreat in the heart of Virginia. Every summer artists gather here for three weeks of work unencumbered by commercial producers, indoor plumbing, or union schedules. Robert Graham Small is the gifted play and screenplay guru for this unusual and tenacious company.

WHO: Any playwright or screenwriter.

STAFF: Robert Graham Small, Director

APPLICATION: Two copies of script and statement of your background.

ADDRESS: ShenanArts, Route 5, Box 167-F, Staunton, VA 24401.

The Sundance Playwrights Laboratory

The Center for Performing Arts at Sundance (Robert Redford, founder) offers the Playwrights Conference every summer. This program is designed to advance the skills and artistry of selected playwrights by allowing them to work with collaborators they choose. The program is held for a month at the Sundance Resort in Provo Canyon, Utah.

WHO: Playwrights and collaborative teams of directors, dramaturges, actors, composers, etc.

STAFF: David Chambers, Executive Director

APPLICATION: Scripts must be submitted by a producer or literary manager.

ADDRESS: Box 16450, Salt Lake City, UT 84116.

Playwrights' Retreats

In reading through the workshop descriptions you'll note that very few programs currently offer more than a two-week residency. The trend toward getting playwrights together to bounce ideas off of each other and hear each other's work has faded away so that most programs now work with one playwright at a time. We feel that it is important for writers to work together in an ongoing way, and it is worthwhile to note that there are more residency opportunities available for playwrights now than at any time in the recent past. Here are some that we recommend (write for guidelines for all of them):

Altos de Chavon

Residencies of three to four months in the Dominican Republic for fifteen artists each year who can speak Spanish. Minimal fee involved.

APPLICATION: Send letter, résumé, and work sample.

DEADLINE: July 1

ADDRESS: c/o Parsons School of Design, 2 West 13th Street #707, New York, NY 10011.

Mary Anderson Center for the Arts

One-week to three-month residencies in this sylvan retreat right outside Louisville, Kentucky.

APPLICATION: Completed application with project description, work sample, résumé, and two references.

DEADLINE: Ongoing

ADDRESS: 101 St. Francis Drive, Mount St. Francis, IN 47146.

Samuel Beckett Playwriting Internship

Ten-week residency at a very good professional theater in Gloucester, Massachusetts, run by Israel Horovitz. (Most of the theaters in this book offer internships and many include playwrights. This program happens to be one of the most formal playwriting internship programs we know about.)

APPLICATION: Twenty-page writing sample, résumé, and references.

DEADLINE: March 1

ADDRESS: Gloucester Stage Company, 267 East Main Street, Gloucester, MA 01930.

Bellagio Study and Conference Center

Four-week residencies in the Italian Alps.

APPLICATION: Write for brochure and application form.

DEADLINE: Four times a year, apply a year ahead of time.

ADDRESS: The Rockefeller Foundation, 420 Fifth Avenue, New York, NY 10016.

Camargo Foundation

Four- to five-month residencies in Italy, in an ancient Mediterranean fishing town with up to fourteen other artists.

APPLICATION: Completed application form, bio, and three letters of support.

DEADLINE: March 1

ADDRESS: 64 Main Street, Box 32, East Haddam, CT 06423.

Dorset Colony for Writers

One-month or longer residencies in southern Vermont.

APPLICATION: Query letter spelling out project and desired length and time of stay, résumé.

DEADLINE: Open

ADDRESS: Box 529, Dorset, VT 05251.

The Tyrone Guthrie Centre

Three-week to three-month residencies at the estate of legendary theater director Tyrone Guthrie.

APPLICATION: Write for application.

DEADLINE: Ongoing

ADDRESS: Annaghmakerrig, Newbliss, County Monaghan, Ireland.

Hawthornden Castle International Retreat for Writers

Residencies of four weeks at medieval castle in Scotland.

APPLICATION: Write for application.

DEADLINE: September 30

ADDRESS: Lasswade, Midlothian, EH18 1EG, Scotland.

Heartland Plays

Rural Minnesota residencies of two weeks to two months, includes reading of work-in-progress in one or more locales.

APPLICATION: Write for application form.

DEADLINE: January 31

ADDRESS: RR1 Box 245, Browerville, MN 56438.

New York Mills Arts Retreat and Regional Cultural Center

Five to eight writers, musicians, or visual artists are chosen for one- to four-week residencies in this northern Minnesota community where arts define life. (They pay $400 a week stipends plus provide housing.)

APPLICATION: Application form, letters of recommendation for finalists.

DEADLINE: Applications reviewed in June and January.

ADDRESS: 24 North Main Avenue, New York Mills, MN 56567.

Ragdale Foundation

Two-week to two-month residencies at prairie estate near Lake Forest, Illinois.

APPLICATION: Send SASE for application.

DEADLINE: January 15 and June 1

ADDRESS: 1260 North Green Bay Road, Lake Forest, IL 60045.

CHAPTER FIVE

STARTING A NEW PLAY WORKSHOP

Do it yourself, it's the American way.

—Megan Terry

Perhaps there is no theater in your area that is interested in working with new plays. Or the theaters in your area that are interested in new plays either have enough of them or else they want finished "perfect" plays, not plays that need non-performance or reading work.

Then, like Megan Terry, you might want to consider starting a new play workshop. Every one of the programs that we discussed at the end of the last chapter was started by one or more playwrights who felt the need for just such a workshop. Sometimes this is a very personal, even selfish need. Or it may be an interest in serving the broader theater community (e.g., in Minneapolis the playwrights who founded the Playwrights' Center all felt that there was a burgeoning of playwriting talent in the state of Minnesota in the late 1960s but there were no resources that allowed those writers to work).

No longer must you move to New York once you begin to feel that you are becoming a playwright. In fact, many playwrights are doing just the opposite. Once they have had some success as writers for the stage, they move out of New York and back into other regions. Probably the only aspect of living outside of New York City that can be detrimental to a playwright's career is the fact that he or she often loses touch with sympathetic actors and directors. It is important to have access to people who can provide a workshop setting like the ones we described in the last chapter. We hope you noted that many of these currently functioning workshops have grown out of academic programs. Either a university department or playwrights within a university system have decided to get the workshop started, and it has grown into a full-fledged playwrights' workshop. This serves as proof as to how easy it is to establish a playwriting workshop.

For the sake of this chapter we'll define two types of workshops—one that is formal and more of an organization, and one that is very informal and personal. We'll explore ways of setting up each type, and then touch on an even more aggressive position for the playwright—self-producing.

Setting Up a Formal Workshop

Looking back historically to the great periods of playwriting, writers wrote for specific actors, for companies they were part of, for stages that they helped design and build and manage. Those periods provided us with the plays that make up most of our theatrical heritage. The formal workshops of the 1990s offer writers the atmosphere and inspiration of those golden periods. If you are seriously interested in making this age "golden," you should consider starting your own workshop to showcase your plays and the plays of other talented writers. If you work well in groups, the excitement of being surrounded by other talented theatrical people will serve as an inspiration to you. Certainly, such an environment was useful to Shakespeare.

So, by yourself, or with a group of playwrights or other individuals working in theater, you would like to consider starting a formal playwriting workshop. What next? The following information is not meant to be a step-by-step guide as to how to do this, but rather it should serve as an overview of what you should expect to encounter as you begin to organize the workshop.

First of all, it should be decided whether nonprofit status should be applied for. If the workshop is to serve a certain group of playwrights for a limited period of time (say a season or a year or two), then it would be much easier to find another existing nonprofit agency to be a fiscal agent. Colleges, already established theater companies, museums, and so on, can serve this function. By having a fiscal agent, a workshop can accept contributions and grants and save on things such as postage (for bulk mail) and supplies, while at the same time keeping the board of directors informal and the bylaws or rules of the organization flexible.

If the workshop being set up will last longer than a year or two, steps should be taken early on to apply for nonprofit status. It can be very complicated to apply for this status once the organization has been functioning for any lengthy period of time, so it is best to start thinking as soon as possible about taking the necessary steps to setting up as a nonprofit workshop, if that is the direction planned.

Key components of any nonprofit organization include having a board of directors. This board must have at least three members who are unpaid and are not active in the organization in any capacity other than as board members. It helps to get a lawyer, an accountant, and perhaps another nonprofit arts administrator involved in the board early on, because they can help with the mechanics of setting up a board. The second important step for setting up a nonprofit workshop is the establishment of bylaws. Any lawyer will have recommended forms for bylaws. These forms ask for specific information, such as names of board members, how many times a year the organization's board will meet, purpose of the organization, and so on.

Once the board and the bylaws are set up, then application has to be made to the state government to register as a nonprofit organization. This procedure varies from state to state. In New York, the process can take up to a year and involves much scrutiny from the Attorney General's office. In many midwestern and southern states it literally means sending your name in to make sure that no other organization has registered under that specific name. After the state accepts your workshop as a nonprofit organization, then application is made to the Internal Revenue Service. This is usually the most complicated step in the formation of a nonprofit company. If you have a lawyer on your board or know a lawyer willing to give advice, it is best to ask for his or her help at this point, if you haven't already. From the IRS' point of view, they need to determine if you are indeed a nonprofit organization, and, once again, if you are just starting out, it is easier to prove this than if you have been operating for a period of time.

This takes care of the technical problems in setting up a workshop, but there is a more important question: How is it that an artistic structure is put together to best serve the writers, and at the same time prevent the workshop from being just another producing organization that puts itself in a position of saying "no" to playwrights rather than "yes"?

Probably the most important decision concerns the question of producing. It is very difficult for a playwrights' workshop to be a pure workshop and a producing theater as well. The temptation is to do full productions, especially in the first years when income is needed (as in box office) and the number of writers being served is small. If the goal is to be an ongoing and vital workshop serving a large number of writers, then a decision should be made not to produce plays, but to have readings of plays.

Once the decision to produce or not has been made, then

the next decision involves the selection of which playwrights will participate. The various centers and organizations around the country are equally divided on this issue. Half of them are open to any playwrights who meet minimal requirements and take the time to sign up, come to meetings, and perhaps pay nominal dues or an initiation fee. The other half work with committees or a staff that makes selections as to whom they will or will not work with. The one type of workshop becomes almost like a writers' co-op or club, the other like a professional organization. Each type of organization has certain strengths and weaknesses. The professional workshop will in the long run be able to raise more funds in grants, because foundations and government sources will be impressed that the choices are based on artistic criteria. The open-admissions process makes it easier to raise money at the start (usually from members or friends), and the ongoing administrative tasks can usually be divided up among the members because of the collective spirit.

The actual artistic process should include readings of new plays and works-in-progress by professional actors. The better the actor, the more likely it is that the playwright will have a chance to evaluate the script and the work that needs to be done on it. Informal after-the-reading critiques and/or formal panels can be used, with member writers and outside professionals discussing the play with the author. Audiences are important for feedback, but the more time the playwright can spend working with the actors and a good director, the better the workshop experience will be, not only for the playwright but for all concerned.

The rule of thumb in setting up a formal playwrights' workshop is that the playwright should be served. He or she is more important than the audience, the funding sources, the actors, the board, or the fiscal agent. This may seem to be impractical, especially when the rent is overdue or the fiscal agent is threatening to withdraw its funding.

Without a conviction on the part of the workshop to serve

the playwright, there is no chance for the organization to be helpful in any sort of an ongoing, meaningful way. We guarantee that if you talked with the individuals involved in running any of the workshops described in the last chapter, you'd find one common principle that they all share, no matter how diverse their formal organizational structure is: that their mission, as an individual organization and as a collective group, is to "serve the playwright."

> New Dramatists is dedicated to finding gifted playwrights and giving them the time, the space, and the tools to develop their craft, so that they can reach their full potential and make lasting contributions to the theatre.
>
> —Mission Statement,
> New Dramatists

> The purpose of Playwrights Unltd. is to involve, educate and serve playwrights, emerging and established, and other theatre artists, as well as students of theatre, by providing an arena for the development of new work.
>
> —Mission Statement,
> Bay Area Playwrights Festival,
> of Playwrights Unltd.

Setting Up an Informal Workshop

Maybe you aren't interested in filing forms with the IRS, and perhaps you would simply like to start a workshop so that you can get a terrific reading for the plays *you* write. Then the informal workshop is for you.

An informal, or personal, workshop is a workshop set up (usually by the playwright) to help develop a play in the nonperformance workshop setting. Theater is a collaborative process, and sooner or later a writer must place his or her work into the hands of the actors and the director, who will be responsible for seeing that the play gets a full production. If none of the theaters or workshops near you can work with your play for whatever reason (they don't understand it, they don't have time in their schedule, whatever), then you should consider setting up a workshop for work on your play.

How do you go about setting up a workshop? First, and perhaps most important, is selecting a director:

1. You want a director who is experienced in working not only with plays, but with new plays. This person should have a good enough track record that he or she can draw on talented actors to work with the script in the personal workshop.
2. You want a director who is intelligent about the play. You don't want someone who is so supportive that he or she will fail to ask the right questions of you in a workshop setting; at the same time, you need to have a director who understands the script (and, if possible, you as a writer) well enough to be a driving force in the workshop.
3. You want a director who is interested in the script. Some directors say they can direct anything, and some say they do better when they don't care for the play. For a developmental workshop, this won't work. The director must have enough interest in the play to feel that he or she has a stake in its progress and development.

Where do you find directors if you know no one? If you live in an area that has a theater of any type, or, better yet, a playwrights' workshop, then try there. Attend readings and productions, introduce yourself to people, leave a note on a message board if there is one, and, if all else fails, place an ad in a newspaper. There are more directors in the world than there are playwrights. Thus the law of averages states that you will be successful in finding a director, so keep at it. Once you find the director, then the shaping of the workshop should take place.

In creating a personal workshop, use your director. Directors are experienced in working with plays and actors. Even though 6:00 A.M. may be your most creative hour, a sensible director will probably suggest a more convenient time for getting a good group of actors together for work on your play. You may feel that you need a full musical score to back up your second act, but a good director should be able to work out a compromise for the workshop that will give you and all the participants a sense of what is necessary for further work on the play. Once you get a rough schedule of what you want to accomplish, how you will do it, and when you will do it, then you can start plugging actors into your personal workshop.

How do you find your actors? Again, frequent the theaters and workshops near you. Ask your director to recommend people, run an ad, or place a note on a theater's message board. If you can indulge yourself and be selective, hold an audition. Explain carefully to the actors that you are not doing a full production, but rather, you are setting up a workshop and the purpose is to help you realize the potential of your play. If you do hold an audition, look for intelligent actors who are able to read and understand not only the script, but also their own characters. An actor who asks good questions in the right way is well worth any rescheduling you might have to do to accommodate him or her.

Once you have your cast set and your schedule reworked and are ready to go, then find a room that is adequate for work. A living room is not usually the best place for this. Instead you need to have a room with good ventilation, plenty of ashtrays, a table for table work, and a floor area large enough to allow for movement.

A cautionary note from the chapter on cold and staged readings and nonperformance workshops should be repeated at this time. It is tempting to want to move beyond the boundaries of the workshop and do a full production. Make sure that everyone involved understands what your specific goal is and resist the temptation to do more than you should.

A workshop is intended for developing your play to the point where it is ready for production. If you feel you have gotten to that point and you still haven't found someone to produce your play, be patient—it can take time. *The Elephant Man* spent seven years being rejected by some thirty-odd theaters before it was produced, but when it was produced, that production was the right one, and the show moved to New York and then to Broadway, where it became the play of the year. Do read on, because the next section deals with producing your own play—a treacherous journey, but one that many playwrights are involved in.

A Few Words About Producing Your Own Play

More and more playwrights are starting to produce their own work. As the visions of our playwrights get larger and larger in terms of defining what theater is, many playwrights can no longer comb through a list of producers and theaters and find one that might take a chance on their work—let alone produce it. Also, some playwrights, quite selfishly, feel they are entitled to a larger percentage of the profits from a show, so they turn to self-producing. (See page 230 for a breakdown of what a playwright actually gets as a percentage of the gross or as a royalty for production.)

First, let's examine who the producer is. He or she is the driving force behind a full production. Producers raise the necessary funds to do the show, they match up playwright with director and actors with play. They work out contracts for services that are clear and legal, and leave no part of the creative process undefined. The actual physical management of the production is overseen by the producer, both in terms of getting the various design elements done, and in terms of making sure the theater space itself is adequate. Publicity, promotion, defense of and creating enthusiasm for the show are all part of the producer's concerns. Finally, it is the producer's job to evaluate the creative process. Is the play ready to open? Does the second act need work? Is an actor wrong for a role? A director not suited for the play? A play overpowered by its design? A play lessened by its publicity? An audience not clear about the meaning of the play?

This last set of responsibilities is what determines whether or not a playwright should produce his or her own play. A person who is very experienced in the theater may be able to produce his or her own work. That person must surround himself or herself with the best possible people, and these people must have a clear understanding of their responsibilities. The inexperienced will fail, and often fail on more than one account. The naive won't know they are failing, but will fail nevertheless, and the person who is serious about playwriting will best turn to a real producer.

As we note later on, those "real producers" are getting harder and harder to find in the American theater. So if you feel that you're ready to produce your own play and you've tried every avenue to get a production, then remember the first rule of producing. Producing is your number one responsibility. Once you commit to producing your own work, then playwriting must take a backseat to the work that has to be done as a producer. Make sure monies have been raised to cover your costs. Make sure time and budget allocations are adequate for publicity and marketing. Get those reviewers in. Invite the producers you wish would have produced your play. Maybe they'll offer you a theater to extend your run or remount your play, or offer to produce your next script. In the nineties producing your own work is not as much of a no-no as it was in earlier decades. The times have indeed been changing when it comes to theater.

There are a few stories of playwrights pulling a *Rocky*—

producing, writing, and directing their own scripts when no one else will touch them. There are many more stories about a play or playwright with potential that never realized that potential because of a second-rate initial production of a play which the playwright produced.

CHAPTER SIX

ENTERING CONTESTS

> The Actors' Theatre of Louisville's Great American Play Contest has probably become the most positive producing force behind new plays in America today. And they're nice people too.
>
> —John Pielmeier, author of *Agnes of God*

Contests are an excellent way for a totally unknown playwright to suddenly become known. Theater is a very image-conscious business and winning a contest gets publicity for both you and your play, and that helps to get your script to the top of that pile of scripts which every producer, every regional theater has sitting around waiting to be read.

If applying for grants as an individual playwright is somewhat like choosing a number in a lottery, then sending scripts to a contest is much the same as playing a slot machine. There are literally hundreds of contests in any given year for playwrights. Some of these are very worthwhile, and winning these contests (or even finishing among the finalists) can lead to workshopping and even full production experiences. We have selectively picked contests that are very good for playwrights to enter. Please keep in mind that there are many others as well.

But before you submit a play, take the time to study the following guidelines. Anyone who runs a playwriting contest will tell you that at least forty percent of the plays they receive are submitted improperly or are simply not eligible for the contest. The cost of paper, envelopes, and postage can add up, plus submitting material eats up valuable writing time. Don't make your life as a playwright more difficult by not paying attention to contest guidelines.

Commonsense Guidelines

Commonsense Guideline #1. Take the time to read about contests. Here are three publications that list contest information.

Dramatists Sourcebook $9.95
Theatre Communications Group, Inc.
355 Lexington Avenue
New York, NY 10017

The Writer Magazine $17.00/year subscription; $1.50/issue
8 Arlington Street
Boston, MA 02116

The Dramatists Guild Newsletter
(free with membership)
The Dramatists Guild, Inc.
234 West 44th Street
New York, NY 10036

Commonsense Guideline #2. Unless the deadline is tomorrow, don't simply send your manuscript to a contest. Spend 64 cents to send a self-addressed stamped envelope (SASE), requesting more information about the contest. Many contests have detailed rules sheets and many of them require a simple entry form to be filled out. The SASE is a courtesy that helps ensure your quickly receiving information and, if necessary, an application form.

Commonsense Guideline #3. Send a cover letter with your material. Here is a format that works for most script submissions to a contest. It doesn't have to be lengthy, but it should explain what is in your envelope.

April 14, 1996

Ms. Marcina Motter
Literary Manager
National Play Award #405
630 North Grand Avenue
Los Angeles, California 90012

Dear Ms. Motter,

Enclosed please find a copy of my full-length play ______________________________. I am submitting this script to you as an entrant for the National Play Award. This play has never had a professional production. An earlier draft was given a chamber reading at the Shenendoah International Playwrights Retreat in Virginia.

I have also enclosed a SASE for the play's return. If you or one of your staff could take a moment to return the enclosed postcard I would appreciate it.

Thanks to you and the National Play Award for encouraging playwrights in this way.

Sincerely,

enc: script
SASE
stamped postcard

Commonsense Guideline #4. Do send an SASE. Most contests—and rightfully so—have a rule that they won't return scripts without a return envelope. And get to know the post office's various rates so your envelope has the proper amount of postage, together with a clear indication of what class you want to send it. Fourth Class is acceptable for a manuscript, but you have to add First Class postage for the cover letter, and you have to be patient. First Class is more expensive, but you get your manuscript back within a week to ten days of when it is mailed in your SASE.

Commonsense Guideline #5. You don't usually have to send an acknowledgment postcard, but many contests prefer that you do. Send a postcard of receipt together with your cover letter, SASE, and script. A typical format for this postcard is as follows:

> ____________________
> (Date)
>
> ____________________ has received your
> (Name of Contest, Theater)
> manuscript and will be getting back to you when our judges have made their final decisions.

Put your name and address on the front along with the postage. The post office sells postcards with postage already on them.

Commonsense Guideline #6. Most contests deal with as many as 100 to 2,500 scripts. These usually come in at about the same time—the deadline. Don't call to ask if the script arrived. Don't even write to ask the same question. If you are worried, send the acknowledgment postcard; otherwise, be patient. No theater that runs a contest has a staff large enough to handle your individual query—especially near the deadline.

Commonsense Guideline #7. Don't attempt to change your manuscript after you have submitted it—for the reason listed above concerning staff time, but more important, because of the way most contests are structured, within days of receipt of your submission readers are already starting to judge your work. Thus sending in a new first act a month after the deadline, or deciding you don't like the play you submitted and trying to send a new one in will get you nothing but the focused frustration of the contest staff.

Commonsense Guideline #8. If you are entering more than one script in a contest (and check to make sure this is allowed), use separate envelopes, separate SASEs, separate acknowledgment postcards, and separate cover letters. Again, remember that the volume of mail that has to be processed can be very large, and anything you can do to help will be appreciated.

Commonsense Guideline #9. If more than one category is open for submission in a contest (i.e., "musical comedies," "children's plays," "one-acts"), clearly indicate in both your cover letter and on the outside of your submission envelope under which category the enclosed script is entered.

Commonsense Guideline #10. If you are not a winner of the contest, don't resubmit the same play in the same contest unless it has undergone major rewrites and you know it is all right to do so. But within this same guideline, if you have a new script or you have done considerable rewrites (and the contest allows you to resubmit these), do send in your script the next time the contest is offered. Many contests use judges as readers who have read for them before, and if they are impressed with your writing, they might be on the lookout for your material in a subsequent year. (Or if they see a vast improvement from one year to the next in your submissions, they also might try to reward that improvement.)

Generally, it is better to avoid contests (or reading services, for that matter) which charge a large (e.g., over $25) fee. Playwriting contests are intended to help encourage the writing of plays and to give exposure to unknown playwrights. If the contest charges a high entry fee, profits are obviously being made from the competition, so writers should save their money, postage, and time by not entering.

Contests

American Shorts Contest

AWARD AMOUNT: $500 and production expenses (also production awards).

FREQUENCY: Annual

ELIGIBILITY: Any American playwright.

GUIDELINES: Play of five or fewer pages. Held at one of the best Southern theaters for new works, this contest is a great first contest to enter.

APPLICATION PROCEDURE: Write for more information (send SASE), as each year one or more themes are announced.

ENTRY FEE: None

DEADLINE: June 15

NOTIFICATION: Early fall

ADDRESS: Florida Studio Theatre, 1241 North Palm Avenue, Sarasota, FL 34236.

Baker's Plays High School Playwriting Contest

AWARD AMOUNT: First prize: $500 and publication; Second prize: $250; Third prize: $100.

FREQUENCY: Annual

ELIGIBILITY: Any playwright in high school.

GUIDELINES: One-act or full-length play for young audiences that has had a production or public reading.

APPLICATION PROCEDURE: Full script plus letter from high school teacher who will sponsor entry; write for additional information.

ENTRY FEE: None

DEADLINE: January 31

NOTIFICATION: May

ADDRESS: 100 Chauncy Street, Boston, MA 02111.

Beverly Hills Theatre Guild—Julie Harris Playwright Award

AWARD AMOUNT: First prize: $5,000 plus $2,000 to help finance an L.A. production; Second prize: $2,000; Third prize: $1,000.

FREQUENCY: Annual

ELIGIBILITY: U.S. citizen who hasn't won a major prize.

GUIDELINES: Unproduced, unpublished, unoptioned play. Write for guidelines.

APPLICATION PROCEDURE: Script and entry form.

ENTRY FEE: None

DEADLINE: November 1

NOTIFICATION: June

ADDRESS: 2815 North Beachwood Drive, Los Angeles, CA 90068.

Dubuque Fine Arts Players National One-Act Playwriting Contest

AWARD AMOUNT: First prize: $600; Second prize: $300; Third prize: $200; Possible production for all three winners.

FREQUENCY: Annual

ELIGIBILITY: U.S. citizens.

GUIDELINES: One-acts no longer than forty minutes in length. Send SASE for information and mandatory application form.

APPLICATION PROCEDURE: Entry form, two copies of script, one-paragraph synopsis, and optional SASE.

ENTRY FEE: $10 per submission

DEADLINE: January 31

NOTIFICATION: June

ADDRESS: 569 South Grandview Avenue, Dubuque, IA 52003.

Emerging Playwright Award

AWARD AMOUNT: $500, production, travel expenses to attend rehearsals.

FREQUENCY: Annual

ELIGIBILITY: Minority playwrights encouraged, but any developing playwright can apply.

GUIDELINES: Full-lengths and one-acts, unproduced in New York City.

APPLICATION PROCEDURE: Script with production history and bio.

ENTRY FEE: None

DEADLINE: Ongoing

ADDRESS: Playwrights Preview Productions, Box 1019, Lenox Hill Station, New York, NY 10021.

Lawrence S. Epstein Playwriting Award

AWARD AMOUNT: $250

FREQUENCY: Annual

ELIGIBILITY: Any American playwright.

GUIDELINES: Unproduced full-length or bill of related one-acts.

APPLICATION PROCEDURE: Script only. (Epstein's heart is in the right place; he is truly trying to encourage writers for the stage and makes this as painless as possible.)

ENTRY FEE: $1 optional

DEADLINE: March 31

NOTIFICATION: December

ADDRESS: 115 Hatteras Road, Barnegat, NJ 08005-2814.

John Gassner Memorial Playwriting Award

AWARD AMOUNT: First prize: $500, staged reading, and possible publication; Second prize: $250.

FREQUENCY: Annual

GUIDELINES: Unproduced and unpublished full lengths. One submission per writer. Play must not be under option for production or publication.

APPLICATION PROCEDURE: Submit three copies of script. Script must include cover page, cast list with character descriptions, brief synopsis, and statement that play has not been published or produced and is not under option.

ENTRY FEE: $10 for non–New England Theatre Conference members

DEADLINE: April 15

NOTIFICATION: September

ADDRESS: NETC c/o Department of Theatre, Northeastern University, 306 Huntington Avenue, Boston, MA 02115.

Gilman and Gonzalez-Falla Theatre Foundation Musical Theatre Award

AWARD AMOUNT: $25,000

FREQUENCY: Annual

ELIGIBILITY: Must have had a musical produced by a commercial or nonprofit theater.

GUIDELINES: Write for more details (definitely worth applying for if you are eligible).

APPLICATION PROCEDURE: See guidelines.

ENTRY FEE: None

DEADLINE: TBA

ADDRESS: 109 East 64th Street, New York, NY 10021.

The Little Theatre of Alexandria National One-Act Playwriting Competition

AWARD AMOUNT: First prize: $350 and possible production; Second prize: $250; Third prize: $150.

FREQUENCY: Annual

ELIGIBILITY: U.S. citizens.

GUIDELINES: Unpublished and unproduced play with running time under sixty minutes and requiring only one set. Send SASE. (One of the most venerable competitions for one-acts.)

APPLICATION PROCEDURE: Script with character descriptions and synopsis.

ENTRY FEE: None

DEADLINE: March 31

NOTIFICATION: September/October

ADDRESS: 600 Wolfe Street, Alexandria, VA 22314.

Love Creek One-Act Festivals

AWARD AMOUNT: Showcase for up to forty playwrights a year in New York City. $300 for best play of each mini-festival.

FREQUENCY: Annual

GUIDELINES: Unpublished play, unproduced in New York City in last year, cast of 2 or more, 40 minutes or less in length. Send SASE for detailed information on the many mini-festivals and showcases this active company does each year.

APPLICATION PROCEDURE: Send up to two plays with a letter giving theater permission to produce play under AEA showcase code.

ENTRY FEE: None

DEADLINE: Several a year

NOTIFICATION: 6 weeks to 6 months

ADDRESS: 47 El Dorado Place, Weehawken, NJ 07087-7004.

Mixed Blood Versus America

AWARD AMOUNT: $2,000 plus production.

FREQUENCY: Annual

ELIGIBILITY: U.S. citizen who has had at least one play produced or workshopped.

GUIDELINES: Unproduced, unpublished work. This is an unusual and interesting contest run by Mixed Blood Theatre, one of Minnesota's most innovative theaters. Write for details.

APPLICATION PROCEDURE: Script with proof of past production or workshop.

ENTRY FEE: None

DEADLINE: March 15

NOTIFICATION: Fall

ADDRESS: 1501 S. 4th Street, Minneapolis, MN 55454.

Nantucket Short Play Competition

AWARD AMOUNT: $200 and one or more staged readings.

FREQUENCY: Annual

GUIDELINES: Any one-act less than forty pages that has not been published or had an Equity production.

APPLICATION PROCEDURE: Send one copy of your play, and a cover letter with name and address, with SASE business envelope and SASE for script return.

ENTRY FEE: $5

DEADLINE: March 1

NOTIFICATION: Late April

ADDRESS: Jim Patrick, Literary Manager, P.O. Box 2177, Nantucket, MA 02584.

Susan Smith Blackburn Prize

AWARD AMOUNT: First prize: $5,000 plus signed Willem de Kooning print; Second prize: $1,000; $500 prizes for eight to ten other finalists.

FREQUENCY: Annual

ELIGIBILITY: Any female playwright who writes in English.

GUIDELINES: Full-length plays, unproduced or produced within one year of deadline. *Must* be nominated by a professional producer, artistic director, literary manager.

APPLICATION PROCEDURE: Submit two copies of play. No submissions by playwrights themselves, but you can contact someone who works with a theater to see if he/she would nominate your work by submitting a letter.

ENTRY FEE: None

DEADLINE: September 20

NOTIFICATION: February

ADDRESS: 3239 Avalon Place, Houston, TX 77019.

L. Arnold Weissberger Playwriting Competition

AWARD AMOUNT: $5,000

FREQUENCY: Annual

ELIGIBILITY: Unpublished and unproduced professionally.

GUIDELINES: Write for information.

APPLICATION PROCEDURE: Script with letter of recommendation from a theater professional.

ENTRY FEE: None

DEADLINE: May 31

NOTIFICATION: The following May

ADDRESS: c/o New Dramatists, 424 West 44th Street, New York, NY 10036.

West Coast Ensemble Contests

AWARD AMOUNT: $500 and production.

FREQUENCY: Annual

GUIDELINES: Full-lengths and musicals with casts of no more than 12, not produced in Southern California.

APPLICATION PROCEDURE: Script with SASE.

ENTRY FEE: None

DEADLINE: December 31 for plays; June 30 for musicals

NOTIFICATION: Within six months

ADDRESS: Box 38728, Los Angeles, CA 90038.

CHAPTER SEVEN

GETTING YOUR PLAY PRODUCED

A famous novelist who asked to remain anonymous said after his one venture into playwriting that "in the theater literature is never finished." In the first half of this book playwrights were warned not to wait too long to let other people see their work. Perfection may never be achieved, no matter how many rewrites you do, and you should start getting feedback from people as early as possible. This doesn't mean you should send your first draft off to a Broadway producer, but it does mean that you should seek input from artistic directors and literary managers who are interested in your work, and it also means that even though you might be a beginning playwright, you should have no fear of submitting your play to a theater company or a producer who is interested in seeing new works.

One warning about feedback. If someone is interested enough in your work to respond—wonderful. Add those responses to other comments you have been gathering through your various readings and workshops, but take heed of the advice that Romulus Linney (author of *Childe Byron*, *FM*, *Tennessee*, etc.) gives:

> Realize that play readers for theatres are the most arbitrary, dogmatic and overworked of all judges of art. If one likes your play, prepare to receive exhaustive and sweeping notions for revisions, and decide whether you will play that game or not. Remember there are three primal urges of human beings: food, sex and rewriting someone else's play.

If you compare the following list of theaters and producers interested in new works with a list from ten or even five years ago, you'll notice two major changes. The number of people and places wanting to read unsolicited work is about a third of what it was a decade ago. But don't get discouraged, as a growing number of theaters and producers now want to see a synopsis of your work along with a sample of the dialogue. One student playwright recently commented: "You go through several drafts of a 120-page play, and then when you think it is getting ready to be read you pick ten pages to mail out!" The second major change is the shrinking number of commercial—as opposed to not-for-profit—producers who will look at unsolicited work. We've decided not to include any of the major producers who'll only look at submissions from agents. If you have an agent they don't need our list, and if you don't have an agent those doors are closed to you unless you can get a producer interested by way of a reading, workshop, or production somewhere else.

Although nonprofit theaters have given writers for the stage many opportunities to have their plays seen, they rarely provide a playwright with enough income to do much more than pay the rent for a month or two. Thus our list starts off with regional theaters—both big and small—and moves to New York City nonprofit theaters, and then to the shrinking list of Broadway and other commercial producers. More and more new works are following the same path: They are first presented in regional theaters, then in nonprofit New York theaters, and finally, for a very select (lucky) few, there are commercial runs in New York City or elsewhere.

Playwrights need to see their work on its feet with lights, sets, and costumes, and in front of an audience. Very important in this process are regional, semiprofessional, or nonprofessional theaters. In many parts of the country, community theaters or experimental non-Equity companies are eager to work with playwrights.

The question you might well ask at this point is which theater/producer should I send my play to? We've tried to give at least one title for each listing, which should suggest what the taste of the producer is or the interest of the audience that the company is serving. To reiterate advice that we started this book with: Do read plays. After you have studied the following lists of theaters and producers interested in reading new plays, be sure to read the plays that these theaters and producers have produced.

Regional Theaters

This is a very eclectic group of theaters. Budgets range from under $100,000 to many, many millions of dollars. For every regional theater that has shut down in the last decade there has been at least one new theater to replace it. These newer, smaller theaters are often more eager to read new writers' works, and that is why we have included some of them. Note that most regional theaters are now asking that you send a synopsis or a query letter instead of sending a play.

Actors' Theatre of Louisville

PAST PRODUCTIONS: *The Gin Game* by D. L. Coburn, *Agnes of God* by John Pielmeier, *Haikku* by Katherine Snodgrass, *Two* by Romulus Linney

GUIDELINES: Unsolicited short plays only—ten minutes or shorter. Longer plays must be recommended by a professional theater. December 1 deadline for short play submissions for contest; more detailed rules available from theater.

FACILITIES: There are two main spaces, a 637-seat thrust stage and a 159-seat modified arena space, but this company can be flexible. We've seen fascinating work in their basement bar and a nearby warehouse.

ADDRESS: 316 West Main Street, Louisville, KY 40202-4218.

COMMENTS: The combination of artistic director/playwright Jon Jory and literary manager Michael Bigelow Dixon makes this theater continue to be one of the country's best for both known and unknown playwrights. It is too bad they no longer accept unsolicited full-lengths, but their short play contest is open to one and all, and winners get full productions in their important annual new play festival.

Alabama Shakespeare Festival

PAST PRODUCTIONS: *Hamlet* by William Shakespeare (as well as most of the rest of his work), *Major Barbara* by George Bernard Shaw, *Hedda Gabler* by Henrik Ibsen

GUIDELINES: After years of doing almost exclusively "classic" works, they have begun to look at new works and have even started a Southern Writers Project to encourage works for young audiences. Send synopsis, dialogue sample, and query letter.

FACILITIES: 750-seat proscenium and flexible 200-plus-seat theaters.

ADDRESS: 1 Festival Drive, Montgomery, AL 36117-4605.

COMMENTS: This professional company has emerged as a powerhouse of the theatrical South in the past few years.

American Stage Festival

PAST PRODUCTIONS: *Agnes of God* by John Pielmeier, *The Voice of the Prairie* by John Olive, *Our Town* by Thornton Wilder

GUIDELINES: Send synopsis, ten pages of dialogue, and query letter with SASE. For musicals, include cassette of two to three songs.

FACILITIES: 500-seat theater.

ADDRESS: Larry Carpenter, Artistic Director, Box 225, Milford, NH 03055-0225.

COMMENTS: Has set up an Early Stages program to encourage playwrights. Looks for compelling stories for the stage that help to foster a new sense of theatrical reality. They develop these stories through a series of readings leading to workshop productions.

Arena Stage

PAST PRODUCTIONS: *The Great White Hope* by Howard Sackler, *Still Life* by Emily Mann, *Jar the Floor* by Cheryl West

GUIDELINES: Synopsis, query letter, and ten pages of dialogue.

FACILITIES: 827-seat main stage, 514-seat second stage, 160-seat and cabaret theaters for smaller works.

ADDRESS: Doug Wager, Artistic Director, 6th and Maine Avenue SW, Washington, DC 20024.

COMMENTS: One of our most venerable of the "majors." Doug Wager has breathed new artistic life into this company, as evidenced by at least two or three new works each season during his tenure and the New Voice for a New America program that focuses on writers of color.

Artreach Touring Theatre

PAST PRODUCTIONS: Almost every major classic for young audiences, plus some thirty new works, many by artistic director Kathryn Schultz Miller.

GUIDELINES: Accepts unsolicited scripts for young audiences, which can tour with three or fewer actors; must be 50 to 60 minutes running time.

ADDRESS: Kathryn Schultz Miller, Artistic Director, 3074 Madison Road, Cincinnati, OH 45209.

COMMENTS: A great way to break into production—doing plays for young audiences. They are challenging to write and, if you're successful, a source of ongoing royalties. Artreach Touring Company and Miller are among the best at this form of touring theater.

Bilingual Foundation of the Arts

GUIDELINES: Unsolicited scripts, full-lengths, translations and plays for young audiences. Hispanic themes or Hispanic writers only.

FACILITIES: 99-seat Little Theatre and some other spaces.

ADDRESS: 421 North Avenue #19, Los Angeles, CA 90031.

COMMENTS: This company has been growing steadily and has become a real force to be reckoned with in California.

Borderlands Theatre

PAST PRODUCTIONS: *The King of the Kosher Grocery* by Joe Minjares, *Real Women Have Curves* by Josefina Lopez

GUIDELINES: Unsolicited work. Prefers full-lengths. Also accepts translations and adaptations.

FACILITIES: 400-seat main stage and 160-seat second stage.

ADDRESS: Barclay Goldsmith, Producing Director, Box 2791, Tucson, AZ 85702.

COMMENTS: Because of, or in spite of, Arizona Repertory Theatre's success over the last decade, there has been an explosion of theater activity in Arizona. This company is the most open to new works and runs an interesting Border Playwrights Project. This project offers up to ten days of work on plays about the border regions of our country or plays that use the border as a metaphor.

California Theatre Center

PAST PRODUCTIONS: *Apollo: To the Moon* by Mary Hall Surface, *Undine* by James Keller and Adras Ranki, *Imagine* by Clayton Doherty

GUIDELINES: Plays for young audiences. Unsolicited manuscripts are fine, as are adaptations and translations.

FACILITIES: 200 seats, proscenium.

ADDRESS: Will Huddleston, Resident Director, California Theatre Center, Box 2007, Sunnyvale, CA 94087.

COMMENTS: One of the most prolific producers of works for young audiences in the country today.

Charlotte Repertory Theatre

PAST PRODUCTIONS: *The D. B. Cooper Project* by John Orlock, *Darwin* by Tom Dunn, *Veronica's Position* by Rich Orloff

GUIDELINES: Full-length plays and translations that have not been professionally produced.

FACILITIES: 400-seat main stage.

ADDRESS: Claudia Covington Carter, Literary Manager, 2040 Charlotte Plaza, Charlotte, NC 28244.

COMMENTS: They have been quietly producing three to five new works a year in a festival format for over a decade. This company captures nicely the spirit and excitement that is Charlotte in the waning years of this century.

Citiarts Theatre

PAST PRODUCTIONS: *Eau Claire Days* by Richard Elliott, *The Good Times Are Killing Me* by Lynda Barry

GUIDELINES: Accepts unsolicited full-lengths and adaptations.

FACILITIES: 203-seat proscenium and 156-seat thrust.

ADDRESS: Richard Elliott, Artistic Director, 1975 Diamond Boulevard A-20, Concord, CA 94520.

COMMENTS: Very good things heard about them.

Delaware Theatre Company

PAST PRODUCTIONS: *Memoir* by John Murrel, *A Walk in the Woods* by Lee Blessing, and *Fences* by August Wilson

GUIDELINES: Accepts unsolicited scripts; February–May is best time to submit.

FACILITIES: 300-seat thrust.

ADDRESS: 200 Water Street, Wilmington, Delaware 19801-5030.

COMMENTS: Artistic director Cleveland Morris writes some of the nicest rejection letters of any artistic director in the country.

Detroit Repertory Theatre

PAST PRODUCTIONS: *Disability: A Comedy* by Ron Whyte, *Fences* by August Wilson, *Bullpen* by Steven Kluger

GUIDELINES: Full-lengths, especially issue-oriented. Cast limit of 12.

FACILITIES: 186-seat proscenium.

ADDRESS: Barbara Busby, Literary Manager, 13103 Woodrow Wilson Avenue, Detroit, MI 48238.

COMMENTS: Nice to see theater doing well in Detroit.

Live Oak Theatre

PAST PRODUCTIONS: *A Texas Romance* by Ellsworth Schave, *Translations* by Brian Friel

GUIDELINES: Accepts unsolicited scripts. Especially like plays dealing with Southwestern themes.

FACILITIES: 250-seat proscenium.

ADDRESS: Amparo Garcis, Literary Manager, 200 Colorado, Austin, Texas 78701-3923.

Mark Taper Forum

PAST PRODUCTIONS: *The Shadow Box* by Michael Cristofer, *Angels in America* by Tony Kushner, *Black Elk Speaks*, adapted by Marley and Sergel

GUIDELINES: Description of work, five to ten pages of dialogue, and letter. Inquire for best times to submit.

FACILITIES: 740-seat main stage and small second stage.

ADDRESS: Gordon Davidson, Artistic Producer, 135 North Grand Avenue, Los Angeles, CA 90012.

COMMENTS: If all of our major theaters devoted the resources that Mark Taper does to staging new works, this country would be a much better place for playwrights to work.

Mill Mountain Theatre

PAST PRODUCTIONS: *Gun Play* by Tom Dunn, *Spontaneous Combustion* by Sherry Kramer, *White Money* by Julie Jensen

GUIDELINES: Unsolicited one acts. With longer plays, send query letter with synopsis and ten pages of dialogue.

FACILITIES: 400-seat main stage and 125-seat second stage.

ADDRESS: 1 Market Square, 2nd floor, Roanoke, VA 24011-1437.

COMMENTS: Jo Weinstein is the literary manager and a good playwright. She and the rest of the staff go out of their way to make you feel welcome with their New Play Competition, Norfolk Festival of New Works, and monthly lunchtime one-act series—a series of readings of one-acts that plays to audiences of 300 to 400!

The New Tradition Theatre

PAST PRODUCTIONS: *"Master Harold" . . . and the Boys* by Athol Fugard, *10 November* by Steven Dietz, *Pandolfo* by Brian Martinson and Michael Novak

GUIDELINES: Minnesota playwrights given preference, but unsolicited full-lengths from any playwright accepted.

FACILITIES: 140-seat flexible space; occasionally uses 600-seat opera house.

ADDRESS: Marni Swing, Literary Associate, 916 West St. Germain, St. Cloud, MN 56304.

COMMENTS: In the heart of Minnesota, one of the real hot-beds for playwrights in this country.

Offstage Theatre

PAST PRODUCTIONS: *How to Say No* by Doug Grissom, *Hot and Cold* by Tom Coash

GUIDELINES: They look for plays set in specific "sites," and then produce the plays in those places (e.g., last year they wanted scripts that were set in a "fitness center or gymnasium"). Write for specific needs.

FACILITIES: Theater without a theater (they will turn almost any place into a performance site).

ADDRESS: William Rough, Artistic Director, P.O. Box 131, Charlottesville, VA 22902.

COMMENTS: A great place to break into getting produced. Interesting approach to doing theater and getting audiences very involved in new works.

World Premiere Theatre

PAST PRODUCTIONS: *3 Love Stories* by Tom Dunn, *Cancer in Laboratory Animals* by Louise Williams, *Water Main* by Susan Bigelow-Marsh

GUIDELINES: Mostly for California playwrights, but they do fully produce at last one non-Californian each season.

FACILITIES: A "pub" theater in the style of London's West End. Seventy seats in a flexible space above the Lost Coast Brewery.

ADDRESS: Susan Bigelow-Marsh, Artistic Director, 615 4th Street, Eureka, CA 95501.

COMMENTS: One writer who has worked with this company says, "Their heart is in the right place." A perfect example of a new, small company that is open to new works by living writers.

New York Theaters

Circle Repertory Company

PAST PRODUCTIONS: *Redwood Curtain* and *Talley's Folly* by Lanford Wilson, *Levitation* by Timothy Mason

GUIDELINES: Professional recommendation or agent submission, no unsolicited scripts.

FACILITIES: 160-seat Greenwich Village theater.

ADDRESS: Austin Pendleton, Co–Artistic Director, 632 Broadway, 6th floor, New York, NY 10012-2614.

COMMENTS: The only company we've included in this book that won't even allow you to submit an unsolicited synopsis, but if you can get a recommendation, the Circle Rep is well worth sending to, as this company has been a home to many American playwrights over the years.

Manhattan Theatre Club

PAST PRODUCTIONS: *Lips Together, Teeth Apart* by Terrence McNally, *The Last Yankee* by Arthur Miller, *Standing on My Knees* by John Olive, *Eastern Standard* by Richard Greenburg

GUIDELINES: No unsolicited scripts; send résumé, cover letter, synopsis, and ten pages of dialogue.

FACILITIES: 299-seat main stage, 150-seat second stage.

ADDRESS: Lynne Meadow, Artistic Director, 453 West 16th Street, New York, NY 10011.

COMMENTS: One of the four or five most important theaters for new works in New York City.

New York Shakespeare Festival

PAST PRODUCTIONS: *A Chorus Line* by Kleban, Hamlisch, Kirkwood, and Dante, *Don Juan* by Constance Congdon, *Fires in the Mirror* by Anna Deavere Smith

GUIDELINES: Script and SASE.

FACILITIES: Four venues at their home in lower Manhattan.

ADDRESS: George C. Wolfe, Producer, 425 Lafayette Street, New York, NY 10003.

COMMENTS: Besides having Broadway director and writer George C. Wolfe at the helm, the literary manager, Morgan Jenness, is one of the best in the country.

Playwrights Horizons

PAST PRODUCTIONS: *The Dining Room* by A. R. Gurney, *The Heidi Chronicles* by Wendy Wasserstein, *Driving Miss Daisy* by Alfred Uhry, *Assassins* by Sondheim and Lapine

GUIDELINES: *Prefers* unsolicited script with résumé and cover letter.

FACILITIES: 145-seat main stage and 70-seat second stage on New York's Theater Row (42nd Street).

ADDRESS: Artistic Director, 416 West 42nd Street, New York, NY 10036-6896

COMMENTS: One of the best places for playwrights to get produced in this country. The spirit of Andre Bishop has moved on to Lincoln Center with him, but this company continues to produce excellent work. They do only new plays and musicals.

Primary Stages Company

PAST PRODUCTIONS: *2* by Romulus Linney, *Better Days* by Richard Dresser, *All in the Timing* by David Ives

GUIDELINES: Plays by American playwrights not previously produced in New York City.

FACILITIES: Two small Off-Off-Broadway theaters.

ADDRESS: 584 Ninth Avenue, New York, NY 10036.

COMMENTS: The "buzz" is on about this company run by a former program director at New Dramatists, Casey Childs.

Second Stage Theater

PAST PRODUCTIONS: *How I Got That Story* by Amlin Gray, *What a Man Weighs* by Sherry Kramer

GUIDELINES: Five to ten pages of dialogue, résumé, and query letter.

FACILITIES: 110-seat Off-Broadway house.

ADDRESS: Box 1807, Ansonia Station, New York, NY 10023.

COMMENTS: Erin Sanders, a very interesting young playwright, is literary manager. This company pioneered the concept that plays can have a "second production" back in the era when almost no one wanted to be second when it came to producing new work.

Producers

Although logic would make you think that the best way to get a play produced is to send it to a producer, this is actually one of the most difficult ways to get your play performed. Many producers will only consider reading plays that have been submitted through an agent (see pages 233–35). If they like your play, they might consider sending it to producers. But frequently, in spite of their enthusiasm for your work, they will suggest that you first have your play performed at a theater before submission to a producer.

But playwrights have been able to get producers to read their work without going through an agent. Note that the newer producers are about the only ones who are accepting unsolicited work these days.

Jay S. Harris

PAST PRODUCTIONS: Brand-new producer

GUIDELINES: "Plays with an edge and a dramatic story line."

ADDRESS: Weissberger Theater Group, 909 Third Avenue, New York, NY 10022.

COMMENTS: This respected theatrical attorney is carrying on the tradition of Arnold Weissberger—one of the most active manager/attorneys from the forties through the sixties—with a new company devoted to producing interesting Broadway and Off-Broadway plays.

Gladys Nederlander

PAST PRODUCTIONS: *Solitary Confinement* by Rupert Holmes, *The Goodbye Girl* by Neil Simon

GUIDELINES: 46-minute (TV-length) one-act plays with three to six characters for adaptation to television. Send a query letter.

ADDRESS: Jesse D. Stovin, Associate Director, 1650 Broadway #1210, New York, NY 10019.

COMMENTS: A rarity—a commercial New York producer interested in one-acts.

Stuart Ostrow

PAST PRODUCTIONS: *La Bete* by David Hirson

GUIDELINES: Send script with SASE.

ADDRESS: P.O. Box 188, Pound Ridge, NY 10576.

COMMENTS: Has a reputation for not being afraid of "big" works (i.e., plays with large casts and massive technical needs).

Philip Rose

PAST PRODUCTIONS: *The Cemetery Club* by Ivan Menchell

GUIDELINES: Send script with SASE.

ADDRESS: 137 West 78th Street, New York, NY 10024.

COMMENTS: Be patient . . . he's an example of a producer who likes to read new work, but takes a long time to do so.

Dudley Riggs

PAST PRODUCTIONS: This producer runs two different production companies in Minneapolis: Brave New Workshop and Instant Theatre Company. Both specialize in satire. His writer alums include Hollywood notables Pat Proft, Nancy Steen, and Fred McGrath.

GUIDELINES: Accepts unsolicited one-acts and revues.

FACILITIES: 250-seat, tiny theater. Plays also tour.

ADDRESS: 2605 Hennepin Avenue South, Minneapolis, MN 55408.

COMMENTS: Not all producers live in New York City, and not all producers want the next Broadway blockbuster. Dudley Riggs lives in the heartland and has carved out a niche for satire that has given hundreds of writers their first breaks in comedy. Resident company of five does most of the work.

There are many other active producers, but they do not read unsolicited work. If you are fortunate enough to get a production or even a reading of your work you should send notice to the big three commercial producers in this country. They might either send a representative to see your work or request to see a copy of the script. These big three producers are:

The Shubert Organization
234 West 44th Street
New York, NY 10036

The Nederlander Producing Company
1564 Broadway
New York, NY 10036

Jujamcyn Company
246 West 44th Street
New York, NY 10036

How to Submit Your Play to Theaters and Producers

The policy for most of the theaters and producers listed in the previous section is subject to change; that is, their policy concerning submission of plays could be revised. It never hurts to submit a query letter first. Unless the theater specifically asks for a detailed query letter, the following will usually suffice:

April 14, 1996

Ms. Bonnie Morris
Co-Artistic Director
The Illusion Theatre
528 Hennepin Avenue
Minneapolis, Minnesota 55403

Dear Ms. Morris,

Could you please send me information about submitting a new, unproduced play to the Illusion Theatre?

I have enclosed an SASE for your convenience in replying.

Sincerely,

Using the responses to your letters of inquiry, together with information gathered from charts such as those presented in this book, develop a "shopping list" for your play. This list should include all of the places that might be interested in your play (based on comments you have read about them and the list of past productions they have done). List these theaters and producers according to which would be your first choice to have your play done by, and so on, and then prepare to submit the play.

Submitting the play to a theater or producer is similar to submitting to a contest except you don't need an entry form, and generally their rules are not as specific as those for an individual contest. The following guidelines should help you in submitting to theaters and producers.

1. Check your sources by writing the query letter. Don't send a play in May when they specifically state no submissions before July 1, etc.
2. Write a cover letter that includes the background of the play and a sentence or two about yourself. Don't go into great detail about you or your script. Let the work speak for itself and for you.
3. It's a sad fact of theater life that many theaters want to see an outline or sample pages of your work rather than the full play. Do two versions of a synopsis. A one-page "summary" that tells how many characters, the theme, the plot, and the length and a five-page "stepping out" outline that breaks the work down by scene as well as action beats.
4. Include enough return postage on the SASE for your play to be returned. Mail the script in an envelope sturdy enough to protect it and with enough postage for it to arrive safely.
5. If you want to know whether the play arrived safely, include an SASE postcard similar to those you send with contest entries.
6. Do NOT call the producer or the theater company. Re-

member that unsolicited manuscripts go into a pile along with all the other plays, and that, depending upon the time of the year and the size of the staff, it could take anywhere from three to six months to get a reply. We are not trying to discourage you, but just to warn you. There is no need to call every month about a play that you haven't heard about. Wait three months and then write a general letter, inquiring about the status of your play. (Know that it is being read in due course, and that if worse comes to worst and you suspect the play has been lost or mishandled, you can complain to the Dramatists Guild and they will—if nothing else—report to all of their members about the troubles you are having with the specific theater.)

The following letter should serve as a guideline as to what you should write when you have waited three months and have had no response:

date

Ms. Jo Weinstein, Literary Manager
Mill Mountain Theatre, 2nd floor
1 Market Square SE
Roanoke, Virginia 24011-1437

Dear Ms. Weinstein,

In May I sent you my play ____________________.
You acknowledged the receipt of the play, and I am interested in knowing if it is still being read or if it was returned and perhaps lost.

Thank you for checking on this for me.

Sincerely,

Name

7. If the theater writes back and says your script is being held for further consideration, know that the theater is doing just that. Their letter is not an invitation for you to start a correspondence with them or to get worried or overly elated. More readers are looking at your work, and the theater will indeed get back to you.
8. If your script comes back with comments that you find useful, a polite thank-you is all right, but don't start a dialogue through the mail about your play unless the literary manager or artistic director is inviting you to do so. (For example, if someone thought your second act was unfinished, don't send reams of paper explaining why you think it is—it won't change anyone's mind about your play. It never does.)
9. If a theater seems interested in seeing more of your work (and usually they will tell you that in a letter accompanying the return of your script), then remember to send them another play when it is ready. Dramaturges and literary managers especially often take an ongoing interest in a writer and they like to see progress being made.
10. Be polite and professional in all of your dealings with a producer or a theater. Theater is a business, and the playwright's job includes presenting the script in a professional manner. The play represents you, and often you won't actually meet a producer or the staff of a theater until they decide to work with you on the script. So the quality of your typing and the manner in which you respond become doubly important in presenting you and your play.

CHAPTER EIGHT

MAKING ENDS MEET The Financial Side of Playwriting

What exactly are the Facts of Life for a Playwright? Are there any ways to combat the bleak, hard realities of playwriting? What jobs will allow the playwright to continue writing while keeping food on the table and a roof overhead?

If this book made you enthusiastic about the process of playwriting and you are encouraged by the role of the playwright in the theatrical world, then let this last chapter serve as a bit of a warning concerning the life-style choices that a playwright must make in order to function in his or her career.

How to Eat and Write at the Same Time

"Those who can, do . . . those who can't, teach . . ."

This oft-quoted maxim comes from one of modern theater's most prolific writers and most energetic teachers and critics, George Bernard Shaw. Most young playwrights who quote the line don't even know who first said it, but nonetheless they try to obey it: They'll support themselves by waiting tables and driving cabs and feel they are being noble. But teach? Never!

Many of our modern-day American playwrights teach to help support themselves while writing. Additionally, more and more playwrights are finding jobs in the theater as either administrators or artists (actors, designers, directors). It is very difficult to make a living in the theater, but there are alternative jobs that can not only support a life-style which is conducive to playwriting, but in many cases actually enhance the playwriting.

The key is to find that position, whether it be academic or administrative or whatever, that allows you time to write and the freedom to pursue a production or workshop opportunity should it be offered to you. Working in the theater or teaching are not the only alternative jobs that can serve this function. Below is a survey taken by the Artist Services department of New Dramatists. It gives a good cross section of what twenty playwrights, ranging in ages from twenty-five to fifty-five, do to help supplement their incomes as playwrights.

How the Playwrights at New Dramatists Make a Living

Lynne Alvarez—Does tarot card readings for $25 an hour. Also does translations of four languages.
Paul D'Andrea—Teaches at a university where he is also associate director of Theatre of the First Amendment.
Sean Burke—Hospital administrator.
Russell Davis—Builds sets and does juggling.
Gus Edwards—Tends bar.
Thomas George—Newspaper writer.
Anthony Giardina—Teaches playwriting workshops.
Valeria Harris—Administrator for nonprofit organizations.
David J. Hill—Interior painting and wallpapering.

Wendy Kesselman—Translator and film writer.
Faizul Khan—Carpentry.
Warren Kliewer—Theater consultant and director.
Emily Mann—Artistic director of McCarter Theater.
James Nicholson—Teaches at a university.
John Olive—Writes for film.
OyamO—Teaches at a university.
Pat Staten—Word-processes manuscripts.
John Wellman—Teaches playwriting and poetry.
August Wilson—Writes and produces for TV and film.
James Yoshimura—Paints, drives a truck, and works as a bartender.

The Successful Playwright

You can make a killing in the theatre, but you can't make a living.—Robert Anderson

For a nonmusical Broadway play, a writer signs a Dramatists Guild standard contract that guarantees up to 10 percent of the show's weekly gross. This is a sliding scale based on the following:

5% or ___ (whichever is greater) of the first $5,000 of the gross weekly box office receipts, plus 7½% or ___ (whichever is greater) of the next $2,000 of such receipts, plus 10% or ___ (whichever is greater) of all such receipts in excess of $7,000.*

(There are other payment options, but this is the one commonly chosen, along with similar figures for out-of-town per-

* The Dramatists Guild, Inc. Minimum Basic Production Contract, copyright 1955, 1961 by Authors League of America, Inc.

formances prior to the New York opening and for preview performances in New York prior to the official opening.)

What do these percentages mean in terms of real dollars? Let's take a look at *Variety*'s weekly grosses for the week of April 10, 1995 (week 46 of the Broadway season). According to *Variety,* the following box office grosses were reported:

Arcadia by Tom Stoppard	$252,246
Having Our Say by Emily Mann	$153,546
The Heiress by Augustus and Ruth Goetz	$197,251
Rob Becker's *Defending the Cave Man*	$ 46,816
Shakespeare's *Hamlet* (previewing)	$172,543

Using the Dramatists Guild standard contract percentages, the following maximum royalties* were paid on those shows for the week of April 19, 1995:

Arcadia by Tom Stoppard	$ 24,815
Having Our Say by Emily Mann	$ 15,331
The Heiress by Augustus and Ruth Goetz	$ 18,686
Rob Becker's *Defending the Cave Man*	$ 3,812
Hamlet	0

A killing is possible, but consider that one of these shows was in previews and none had paid for their up-front production costs yet, so it is quite possible the producers asked the playwright to give up part of his or her royalties to help get the show started right. Thus, the figures are maximums and the reality is that the playwrights (except Shakespeare) all made less than the figures we've estimated. Also note that only *Arcadia* is an original play; *Having Our Say* and *The Heiress*

* These figures are approximate.

are adaptations and *Hamlet*—well, enough said. (Rob Becker's work developed out of his stand-up comedy.)

If you happen to be the author of one of the five shows listed, before rushing to your stockbroker remember that the IRS taxes royalties at a higher rate than regular income. IRS considers royalties to be in the category of capital gains. Also remember that an agent gets up to 10 percent of the author's royalty figure and that often one or more regional nonprofit theaters have residual rights to the play, which means they can take up to 35 percent of the author's royalties for first premiering the play (or commissioning the play to be written, or awarding the play a prize, etc.). Actors and directors who might have been involved have a piece of the playwright's royalties, depending upon what type of contract was signed before the play moved to Off-Broadway. Added to these costs are also attorney's fees (it should be obvious that legal assistance is important for anyone attempting to write plays for the theater) and, in addition, there is a membership fee for the Dramatists Guild. The best bargain of all these costs, by the way!

What Is the Dramatists Guild?

According to Andrew B. Farber, Executive Director, and Peter Stone, President:

> The Guild offers its more than 7,000 members nationwide the following services and activities:
>
> —Use of the Guild's seven contracts, considered the most comprehensive writer's contracts in the world today, and a royalty collection service.
>
> —Counseling on ALL theatrical contracts—regional, workshop, showcase, and dinner theater, as well as Broadway and Off-Broadway.

—Advice on dealings with producers, agents, and motion picture companies.

—The Hotline, a nationwide toll-free phone number for Active and Associate members with business or contract problems that require immediate assistance.

—An annual marketing directory with up-to-date listings on agents, regional, and New York theaters, grants, playwriting contests, conferences, and workshops.

—Two publications—*The Dramatists Guild Quarterly,* a journal which contains articles on all aspects of the theater, and a newsletter, issued ten times a year, with more immediate information of interest to dramatists.

—Symposia and weekend workshops in major cities across the country, led by experienced theater professionals. Past speakers have included Lanford Wilson and Marshall Mason on "The Playwright/Director Relationship"; Lois Berman, Robert Freedman, Robert Lantz, Helen Merrill, Gilbert Parker, Flora Roberts, Janet Roberts, and Audrey Wood on "How to Get an Agent"; and Betty Comden, Sheldon Harnick, Richard Lewine, Stephen Sondheim, and Jule Styne on "The Anatomy of a Theater Song."

—Membership in the Guild's Committee for Women.

—Access to group health insurance.

—Access to a group life insurance program.

—A lovely room available for rent in the heart of the Broadway theatre district. Great for readings, meetings, backers' auditions, and a quiet place to read and work.

—Free and/or discount tickets to plays in New York City.

The Dramatists Guild is the playwright's only protection when it comes to negotiating contracts for royalties, and author's rights, settling disputes with producers, and so on. The cost is $125 a year for (active) voting membership. You must have had at least one professional production of one of your plays to become an active member. Anyone can be an associate member for $75 a year. If you are not a playwright but work in the theater you can be a subscribing member for $50. Recently, the Guild even opened up a student membership for $25 in their ongoing efforts to expand the range and number of playwrights they serve. If you are lucky enough to get a Broadway production the Guild takes 2 percent of your royalty as their fee, but other than that and the annual dues, they take no other fees from their members. For membership information contact: The Membership Office, The Dramatists Guild, Inc., 234 West 44th Street, New York, NY 10036. (212) 398-9366.

How Important Is an Agent?

If you asked twenty playwrights this question you would get twenty answers, ranging from "absolutely essential" to "worthless." Back in the 1950s every playwright had an agent, and agents were deal makers, marriage brokers, confidants, and talent scouts. Audrey Wood describes herself as:

> an authors' agent. . . . Being an author's agent has no precise definition. Broadly put, my work involves locating talented playwrights, wherever and whenever their ability manifests itself, to encourage them to write, either in their earliest stages or as they emerge from the cocoon to create for the professional theater. If they accept me as their representative, I will attempt to guide their careers and see to their business affairs. Hopefully, together we will both enjoy a long and rewarding future.

With a few rare exceptions most agents no longer have the power to be an Audrey Wood. Agents can help guide a career, they can reach those who read for producers that unsolicited manuscripts may never reach, and perhaps most important they can be very helpful once a contract for an option and/or a production has been offered. Agents cannot be your business or personal managers, they can't balance your checkbook for you, they can't serve as your personal dramaturge or as your private window of the post office. There are many good agents and most of them adhere to the professional guidelines set down by their union. This union also publishes a list of current names and addresses. It might be worthwhile to start submitting your material to agents, so do write and get the updated list of literary agents:

Brochure and Directory ($5 plus SASE for 2 ounces):
Association of Authors Representatives
10 Astor Place, 3rd floor
New York, NY 10003

(There is also a good listing in each summer's edition of *The Dramatists Guild Quarterly*, which is free with membership. Listings of agents are also printed in *Literary Market Place* (LMP), mentioned earlier.)

The Dramatists Guild offers seminars about agents on a regular basis. These question and answer sessions are quite popular. Over the years the following comments have been made about this aspect of the business. For playwrights who view agents as both a vision of the promised land and as a mystery that defies description these might be particularly helpful.

"When should a writer seek out an agent?" Howard Rosenstone said: "The proper time to have representation is when a writer has serious potential for a major production. It is not important for writers to have agents when they are in an early stage of development and are working off-off-Broadway or in small regional theaters."

"How do you get an agent interested to you?" Helen Merrill spoke for most of the agents when she said: "I'll only consider a writer who approaches me on an individual basis. I don't want to see a script that is being submitted simultaneously to more than one agent. It helps if a mutual acquaintance

recommends the playwright, but a good query letter sometimes does the trick."

"What do agents do?" Flora Roberts is particularly sensitive to the dramatist's attitude. "We provide a service. We are not in service." By this she meant that an agent's function is not to copy scripts for a playwright and take care of mailing them wherever the playwright feels it is necessary.

"What do agents look for in a playwright, besides talent?" Mary Hardin looks for "mutual respect." Gil Parker spoke of "a willingness to give serious consideration to advice about revisions."

"What is the proper role of the agent in relationship to the lawyer?" "You keep hearing about there being 'gray areas' in a contract," Flora Roberts said. "If the lawyer has drawn the contract correctly, there are no gray areas. The lawyer's job is to make sure it is all black and white."

One anonymous agent who started in the business working with legendary agent Audrey Wood and has been very successful in the thirty-plus years of her career summed up her work in the mid-nineties as "grunt work." She stated, "It is getting harder and harder to place plays, yet the plays are getting better and better."

Over the years every agent we've met has said that getting an agent should not be a substitute for the playwright having meaningful contact with the theatrical community in all its various forms.

Many young playwrights feel that they absolutely must have an agent if their career is to progress. This is not necessarily so, and agents will be the first to tell you that rather than spending a lot of time, energy, and postage submitting your manuscripts to potential agents, you'd be wiser to get involved in a playwriting workshop. Until there is interest in your material from major nonprofit or commercial producers, an agent cannot do a lot for you. To get to the point where you are attracting the interest from producers, you need to work at the writing of material for the stage. And you need to get acquainted with the rules and regulations of the U.S. Postal Service.

What Does the Post Office Have to Do with Playwriting?

Learn a few basic rules about dealing with the post office, and your life as a playwright will be much easier:

—When sending scripts, always send an SASE. If you don't know what an SASE is, then stop right here and take the time to memorize these words. An SASE is a self-addressed stamped envelope.

—Invest in an inexpensive postage scale and keep current on postal rates. Also know that a few years ago, when the Post Office started offering the $3.00 two-day priority mail rate with the *free* red, white, and blue cardboard mailers, playwrights found out that the American government truly did want to help them in their chosen career. These cardboard mailers are much, much better than the old-fashioned manila envelope. $3.00 is such a great rate for whatever you can fit in these mailers that it usually isn't worth it to mail something book or parcel-post rate.

—If you want an acknowledgment that your script has been received, then send along an SAS postcard and go ahead and do the theater's work for them by writing on the back, "Your script has arrived."

—Send your scripts in a good sturdy binder enclosed in a good sturdy envelope. The U.S. mail can be a tortuous journey for a script, and no matter what any reader tells you, a healthy-looking play will be read in a much different way than one that looks like it is ready for the trash can or—worse yet—than one that resembles a script which has been read by tens of thousands of readers.

As a final mailing rule, acquaint yourself with some of the alternative mail services available in this country. UPS offers very good and inexpensive service on mailing manuscripts. If you're in a hurry, Federal Express and similar services can usually get your script there overnight for not all that much more than you'd pay at the post office (for their Express Mail service anyway).

The Copyright Law and You

If the Dramatists Guild is the playwright's best friend, then a close second is the copyright law. All that copyright means is that you are registering your play with the Library of Congress as your work. Once you do this registration (which costs $20 and takes 5 minutes to complete the form), then your work is protected for "the life of the author plus 50 years." To order application forms, call (202) 287-9100. A booklet, Circular R1—*Copyright Basics,* is available for further information.

Copyright Office
Library of Congress
Washington, DC 20559

Young playwrights spend too much money copyrighting everything they write. You needn't do every draft of a play, nor do you need to have your play copyrighted before you start sending the play out. You receive a good deal of protection for your work simply by marking the title page of your manuscript with a ©. Some writers also send a draft of their play to themselves in a registered envelope which they don't open. If there is ever any question about authorship of the script, the registered, unopened envelope can be presented as proof.

How to Make Money

Nonprofit regional theater productions of plays are becoming very important. Not as tightly controlled by the Dramatists Guild, these theaters generally pay about 6 to 6½ percent of the gross, which can mean up to $9,000 for a decent run and usually averages around $6,000. College theaters, community theaters, and high school theaters will usually pay a standard royalty that ranges from $35 to $100 a performance. Off-Off-Broadway contracts range from showcase/no royalty agreements to near Off-Broadway rates. Any of these types of productions can be helpful to the future life of the play, for the play's continued growth and development. Occasionally they can lead to publication of the play by one of the four or five publishers of plays in this country, although, unfortunately, a Broadway, or at least an Off-Broadway, run usually is needed to get a script published.

The nonprofit and college theaters are also becoming much more involved in giving commissions for new works. A sum of $5,000 is considered to be a generous commission by most non-profit theaters, but along with the commission usually goes an implied agreement for a production, and $5,000 up front certainly is much more useful than royalties once the show is established and running well.

Grants

Or How to Find the Money to Buy the Time to Write Your Play and Then How to Buy the Time to Workshop Your Play . . .

Upon "graduating" from the Navy, unknown playwright Robert Anderson (who later wrote *Tea and Sympathy*) set himself up at a desk with a typewriter and two or three important reference books. Included in this sparse work space was a hand-written sign that read: "Remember No One Ever Asked You To Be A Playwright." He has had that sign hanging on the wall in front of him at every work space since that time.

Playwrights were some of the first individuals to receive "grants." In the first Golden Age of playwriting, the Greek period of the fifth century, cities awarded grants to playwrights to allow them to take time away from their work as teachers, politicians, actors, and so on to write a new play. (They also would hold annual drama festivals, and the winning playwright would get a prize that would allow him to consider giving up one of his other professions at least until the next year's contest.)

The Elizabethans granted commissions to playwrights and their companies. These grants of money often coincided with a holiday festival. It was felt that a new play was a wonderful way to celebrate one of these events. *Twelfth Night* is one of the most memorable plays written under such a grant. By the nineteenth century grants were mostly replaced by advances. In America, commercial producers were actively seeking playwrights who could write, and, more important, were willing to write for an advance against royalties. Since time immemorial playwrights have been faced with the problem of how to feed yourself while taking the time to write, then rewrite, then sell, then rehearse, then rewrite, then open your play.

With the demise of commercial producers over the last twenty years has come the disappearance of the "advance against royalties" grant. But what has replaced it—indeed what many experts feel has replaced the commercial producer for playwrights—is the not-for-profit system of giving grants. Today there are many different organizations regularly giving grants to playwrights.

Before we get to a listing of those grants available to playwrights, we think it is important to explain a few rules of the game. The not-for-profit arts world is a very recent twist on the age-old process of subsidizing artists and companies. Before World War II there were a few symphony orchestras and museums that were not-for-profit in this country, but only four theaters. After World War II the numbers of theaters that were not-for-profit began to multiply very quickly, so that in 1994 it was estimated that there were around 480.

What does not-for-profit mean? Just that. The IRS rules that certain theater companies do not make a profit and are thus eligible for support from the general public, from government agencies, and from private foundations and corporations.

Grants

National Endowment for the Arts

The fate of the N.E.A. is being very publicly debated but as of the writing of this book this is where the agency and its important playwright fellowship program stand.

AWARD AMOUNT: One-year fellowships up to $17,500; two-year awards up to $35,000.

FREQUENCY: Bi-annual

ELIGIBILITY: Playwrights who have had a play produced by a professional theater company within the last five years. Must be a citizen or a permanent resident of the United States.

GUIDELINES: Six copies of a play written within the last five years.

APPLICATION PROCEDURE: Request application booklet from office. Will also need up to three letters of reference.

DEADLINE: June 30

NOTIFICATION: March

ADDRESS: Theatre Program Grants Office/TH FEL., National Endowment for the Arts, 1100 Pennsylvania Avenue NW, Washington, DC 20506.

Fund for New American Plays

An example of the many new funding opportunities that have emerged for playwrights in the last few years. This is another good reason to get to know one or more theater companies well, because a theater must apply on behalf of a playwright.

AWARD AMOUNT: $10,000 plus production support (seven were awarded in 1994); $2,500 Roger Stevens Awards (four were given in 1994).

FREQUENCY: Annual

ELIGIBILITY: Playwright must be nominated by theater that wants to produce his or her new play.

GUIDELINES: Write for proposal information.

APPLICATION PROCEDURE: Theater sends script and production budget.

DEADLINE: March 15

NOTIFICATION: September

ADDRESS: The John F. Kennedy Center for the Performing Arts, 2700 F Street NW, Washington, DC 20566.

McKnight Fellowships

The Playwrights Center has become one of the major financial as well as artistic supporters of playwrights. These two grants are just part of their program.

AWARD AMOUNT: $10,000 plus up to $2,000 more for related expenses (two given in 1994).

FREQUENCY: Annual

ELIGIBILITY: U.S. citizen with at least one professional production. Must agree to spend at least two months in-residence in Minnesota. Past fellowship winners may reapply every three years.

GUIDELINES: Fellowships designed to assist professional playwrights and to enrich the artistic life of the Playwrights Center and the state of Minnesota.

APPLICATION PROCEDURE: Request form from Center and do a brief narrative of career history along with a list of production credits.

DEADLINE: December 15

NOTIFICATION: April 15

ADDRESS: The Playwrights Center, 2301 Franklin Avenue East, Minneapolis, MN 55406.

McKnight Advancement Grants

AWARD AMOUNT: $8,500 and up to $1,500 for related expenses (four given in 1994).

FREQUENCY: Annual

ELIGIBILITY: Minnesota resident for at least a year.

GUIDELINES: (same as above)

APPLICATION PROCEDURE: (same as above)

DEADLINE: January 7

NOTIFICATION: April 15

ADDRESS: (same as above)

The Kleban Award

Award established by *A Chorus Line* lyricist Edward Kleban before he passed away.

AWARD AMOUNT: $50,000

FREQUENCY: Annual (alternates yearly between lyricists and librettists)

ELIGIBILITY: Must have had a full or workshop production of at least one work or be a member of ASCAP, BMI, Dramatists Guild, or other recognized musical theater workshop.

GUIDELINES: Awards meant to make a major difference in the careers of musical theater writing artists with proven potential.

APPLICATION PROCEDURE: Sample of work submitted with completed application (write for form).

DEADLINE: TBA

NOTIFICATION: TBA

ADDRESS: Zissu, Stein and Mosher, 270 Madison Avenue #1410, New York, NY 10016.

John Simon Guggenheim Memorial Foundation

In our opinion more playwrights should apply for these fellowships. Artists in other disciplines get a much higher percentage of these important awards than playwrights.

AWARD AMOUNT: Flexible based on budget submitted for fellowship year's needs.

FREQUENCY: Annual

ELIGIBILITY: U.S. citizens who have demonstrated exceptional creative ability.

GUIDELINES: These fellowships can make a big difference in a playwright's career, as they are meant to support a project as well as buy writing time for up to a year.

APPLICATION PROCEDURE: Write for information and application.

DEADLINE: October 1

NOTIFICATION: March

ADDRESS: 90 Park Avenue, New York, NY 10016.

Princess Grace Awards

Established in honor of Princess Grace and meant to encourage younger, developing artists.

AWARD AMOUNT: $7,500

FREQUENCY: Annual

ELIGIBILITY: U.S. citizen or permanent resident under thirty years old.

GUIDELINES: Award based on artistic quality of script submitted and how artist would make use of ten-week residency in New York City.

APPLICATION PROCEDURE: Write for information.

DEADLINE: March 31

NOTIFICATION: June

ADDRESS: Princess Grace Foundation—USA, 725 Park Avenue, New York, NY 10021.

Jerome Fellowships

Another very important grant for developing playwrights.

AWARD AMOUNT: $7,000 for five playwrights.

FREQUENCY: Annual

ELIGIBILITY: A playwright who has not had more than one professional production and who is interested in spending a year in-residence in Minnesota.

GUIDELINES: Application form, script, and résumé.

APPLICATION PROCEDURE: Write for information and form.

DEADLINE: September 15

NOTIFICATION: January 16

ADDRESS: Playwrights Center, 2301 Franklin Avenue E., Minneapolis, MN 55406.

Bunting Fellowship Program

If you're a woman, read on.

AWARD AMOUNT: $30,000

FREQUENCY: Annual

ELIGIBILITY: Women playwrights, composers, and librettists.

GUIDELINES: Must live in Boston area during year of fellowship.

APPLICATION PROCEDURE: Write for application form and submit with $40 fee.

DEADLINE: October 15

NOTIFICATION: April 30

ADDRESS: The Mary Ingraham Bunting Institute of Radcliffe College, 34 Concord Avenue, Cambridge, MA 02138.

Bush Foundation

This program could serve as a model for how a private foundation can give meaningful grants to individual artists.

AWARD AMOUNT: $26,000 plus $7,000 for production and travel expenses.

FREQUENCY: Bi-annual

ELIGIBILITY: Resident of Minnesota, South Dakota, North Dakota, or Western Wisconsin. Must have had at least one professional production and be 25 or older.

GUIDELINES: Available from the Director of Fellowships in the fall of every year.

APPLICATION PROCEDURE: Script and completed application form.

DEADLINE: Mid-October

NOTIFICATION: March

ADDRESS: E-900 First National Bank Building, St. Paul, MN 55101.

Dobie-Paisano Project

Another grant that includes financial support with a residency.

AWARD AMOUNT: $7,200 and six-month residency expenses.

FREQUENCY: Annual

ELIGIBILITY: Playwrights who are native Texans, living in Texas, or now focusing their work in Texas and the Southwest.

GUIDELINES: Available from project office.

APPLICATION PROCEDURE: Completed application form and script.

DEADLINE: March 1

NOTIFICATION: May

ADDRESS: Dobie-Paisano Fellowship, University of Texas at Austin, Main Building 101, Austin, TX 78712.

In closing this section on grants, here's a good suggestion: Write to your state arts council for grant information. The addresses are listed below.

Alabama State Council on the Arts
1 Dexter Avenue
Montgomery, AL 36130-5401
Al Head, Executive Director
(205) 242-4076

Alaska State Council on the Arts
411 West 4th Avenue, Suite 1E
Anchorage, AK 99501-2343
Timothy Wilson, Executive Director
(907) 279-1558

American Samoa Arts Council
Box 1540
Office of the Governor
Pago Pago, AS 96799
Fa'ailoilo Lauvao, Executive Director
(011)(684) 633-4347

Arizona Commission on the Arts
417 West Roosevelt Avenue
Phoenix, AZ 85003
Shelley Cohn, Executive Director
(602) 255-5882

Arkansas Arts Council
1500 Tower Building, 323 Center Street
Little Rock, AR 72201
Bill Puppione, Executive Director
(501) 324-9150

California Arts Council
2411 Alhambra Boulevard
Sacramento, CA 95817
Barbara Pieper, Executive Director
(916) 227-2550

Colorado Council on the Arts
750 Pennsylvania Street
Denver, CO 80203
Barbara Neal, Executive Director
(303) 894-2617

Connecticut Commission on the Arts
227 Lawrence Street
Hartford, CT 06106
John Ostrout, Executive Director
(203) 566-4770

Delaware Division of the Arts
820 North French Street
Wilmington, DE 19899-8911
Peggy Amsterdam, Director
(302) 577-3540

District of Columbia Commission on the Arts and Humanities
410 8th Street NW, 5th floor
Washington, DC 20004
Pamela Holt, Executive Director
(202) 724-5613

Florida Division of Cultural Affairs
Department of State, The Capitol
Tallahassee, FL 32399-0250
Peyton C. Fearington, Executive Director
(904) 487-2980

Georgia Council for the Arts
530 Means Street NW, Suite 115
Atlanta, GA 30318
Caroline Ballard Leake, Executive Director
(404) 651-7920

Guam Council on the Arts & Humanities Agency
Office of the Governor, Box 2950
Agana, GU 96910
Alberto A. Lamorena V, Executive Director
(011)(671) 477-7413

State Foundation on Culture and the Arts (Hawaii)
335 Merchant Street, Suite 202
Honolulu, HI 96813
Wendell Silva, Executive Director
(808) 586-0300

Idaho Commission on the Arts
304 West State Street
Boise, ID 83720
Margot H. Knight, Executive Director
(208) 334-2119

Illinois Arts Council
State of Illinois Center
100 West Randolph Street, Suite 10-500
Chicago, IL 60601
Rhoda Pierce, Acting Executive Director
(312) 814-6750

Indiana Arts Commission
402 West Washington Street, Room 072
Indianapolis, IN 46204
Julie Murphy, Interim Director
(317) 232-1268

Iowa Arts Council
Capitol Complex
Des Moines, IA 50319
William H. Jackson, Executive Director
(515) 281-4451

Kansas Arts Commission
Jayhawk Tower
700 Jackson, Suite 1004
Topeka, KS 66603
Dorothy Ilgen, Executive Director
(913) 296-3335

Kentucky Arts Council
31 Fountain Place
Frankfort, KY 40601
Lou DeLuca, Executive Director
(502) 564-3757

Louisiana Division of the Arts
Box 44247
Baton Rouge, LA 70804
Gerri Hobdy, Interim Director
(504) 342-8180

Maine Arts Commission
55 Capitol Street
State House Station 25
Augusta, ME 04333
Alden C. Wilson, Executive Director
(207) 287-2724

Maryland State Arts Council
601 North Howard Street, 1st floor
Baltimore, MD 21202
Jim Backas, Executive Director
(410) 333-8232

Massachusetts Cultural Council
80 Boylston Street, 10th floor
Boston, MA 02116
Rose Austin, Executive Director
(617) 727-3668

Michigan Council for the Arts & Cultural Affairs
1200 6th Avenue, Executive Plaza
Detroit, MI 48226-2461
Betty Boone, Executive Director
(313) 256-3731

Minnesota State Arts Board
432 Summit Avenue
St. Paul, MN 55102
Sam Grabarski, Executive Director
(612) 297-2603

Mississippi Arts Commission
239 North Lamar Street, 2nd floor
Jackson, MS 39201
Jane Hiatt, Executive Director
(601) 359-6030; -6040

Missouri Arts Council
111 North 7th Street, Suite 105
St. Louis, MO 63101
Anthony Radich, Executive Director
(314) 340-6845

Montana Arts Council
316 North Park Avenue
Helena, MT 59620
Arlynn Fishbaugh, Executive Director
(406) 444-6430

Nebraska Arts Council
Joslyn Castle Carriage House
3838 Davenport
Omaha, NE 68131-2329
Jennifer Severin, Executive Director
(402) 595-2122

Nevada State Council on the Arts
100 South Stewart Street
Capitol Complex
Carson City, NV 89710
Susan Boskoff, Executive Director
(702) 687-6680

New Hampshire State Council on the Arts
40 North Main Street, Phoenix Hall
Concord, NH 03301
Sue Bonaiuto, Executive Director
(603) 271-2789

New Jersey State Council on the Arts
20 West State Street, 3rd floor, CN 306
Trenton, NJ 08625-0306
Barbara Russo, Executive Director
(609) 292-6130

New Mexico Arts Division
228 East Palace Avenue
Santa Fe, NM 87501
Lara Morrow, Director
(505) 827-6490

New York State Council on the Arts
915 Broadway
New York, NY 10010
Mary Hays, Executive Director
(212) 387-7000

North Carolina Arts Council
Department of Cultural Resources
Raleigh, NC 27611
Mary Regan, Executive Director
(919) 733-2821

North Dakota Council on the Arts
118 Broadway, Black Building, Suite 606
Fargo, ND 58102
Patsy Thompson, Executive Director
(701) 239-7150

Commonwealth Council for Arts and Culture
(Northern Marianas Islands)
Box 5553, CHRB
Saipan, MP 96950
Margarita De Leon Guerrero Wonenberg, Executive Director
(011)(670) 322-9982; -9983

Ohio Arts Council
727 East Main Street
Columbus, OH 43205
Wayne Lawson, Executive Director
(614) 466-2613

State Arts Council of Oklahoma
Jim Thorpe Building #640
2101 North Lincoln Blvd.
Oklahoma City, OK 73105
Betty Price, Executive Director
(405) 521-2931

Oregon Arts Commission
775 Summer Street, NE
Salem, OR 97310
Leslie Tuomi, Executive Director
(503) 986-0082

Pennsylvania Council on the Arts
216 Finance Building
Harrisburg, PA 17120
Philip Horn, Executive Director
(717) 787-6883

Institute of Puerto Rican Culture
Apartado Postal 4184
San Juan, PR 00905
Awilda Palau Suarez, Executive Director
(809) 723-2115

Rhode Island State Council on the Arts
95 Cedar Street, Suite 103
Providence, RI 02903-1034
Iona Dobbins, Executive Director
(401) 277-3880

South Carolina Arts Commission
1800 Gervais Street
Columbia, SC 29201
Suzette Surkamer, Interim Executive Director
(803) 734-8696

South Dakota Arts Council
230 South Phillips Avenue, Suite 204
Sioux Falls, SD 57102-0720
Dennis Holub, Executive Director
(605) 339-6646

Tennessee Arts Commission
320 6th Avenue N, Suite 100
Nashville, TN 37243-0780
Bennett Tarleton, Executive Director
(615) 741-1701

Texas Commission on the Arts
Box 13406, Capitol Station
Austin, TX 78711
John Paul Batiste, Executive Director
(512) 463-5535

Utah Arts Council
617 East South Temple Street
Salt Lake City, UT 84102
Bonnie Stephens, Executive Director
(801) 533-5895

Vermont Council on the Arts
136 State Street, Drawer 33
Montpelier, VT 05633-6001
Nicolette Clarke, Executive Director
(802) 828-3291

Virginia Commission for the Arts
223 Governor Street
Richmond, VA 23219
Peggy Baggett, Executive Director
(804) 225-3132

Virgin Islands Council on the Arts
41-42 Norre Gade
Box 103
St. Thomas, VI 00804
John Jowers, Executive Director
(809) 774-5984

Washington State Arts Commission
234 East 8th Avenue
Box 42675
Olympia, WA 98504-2675
Karen Kamara Gose, Executive Director
(206) 753-3860

West Virginia Division of Culture & History
Arts & Humanities Section
1900 Kanawha Boulevard E
Cultural Center
Charleston, WV 25305
Lakin Ray Cook, Executive Director
(304) 558-0240

Wisconsin Arts Board
101 East Wilson Street, 1st floor
Madison, WI 53702
Dean Amhaus, Executive Director
(608) 266-0190

Wyoming Arts Council
2320 Capitol Avenue
Cheyenne, WY 82002
John G. Coe, Executive Director
(307) 777-7742

In Closing . . .

A playwright must combine a writer's sensitivity with a performer's need to entertain, even show off. You must be able to work alone—set goals, create fictitious worlds—and also be able to work with a community of artists who have come together to give your work life.

The Playwright's Handbook has tried to show what writing a play means: not only the process of writing a play but the development of a working script through the collaborative process of theater. Bringing a new play to the stage is an exhilarating adventure, particularly for the playwright. As a playwright you will find probably no greater satisfaction than to see your words fleshed out, to watch your play take on a life of its own.

Welcome to the world of the playwright.